Tell Me
Something Normal

Garone, Matheus
Tell Me Something Normal
1st edition

Library of Congress Control Number: 2022903477

ISBN 978-0-578-29529-9 (paperback)

Published by
Matheus Garone
Palm Springs, California

Editors
Eduardo Santiago and Lynn Jones Green

Cover design
Erin Schmitt

Interior design
Mark E. Anderson

 AquaZebra™
Web, Book & Print Design

www.aquazebra.com

Printed in the United States of America

May 2020

May 9, 2020

> *She's a wonderful young woman, Katie.*
> *She tested very good for a long period*
> *of time, and then all of a sudden today*
> *she tested positive...*

I turn up the TV so my mom can hear from the kitchen. "Mom! Trump!"

> *She hasn't come into contact with me,*
> *but she spent some time with the vice*
> *president...*

My mom sits down next to me on the couch and offers me a bowl of peeled jackfruit.

"Ew, no."

> *This is why the whole concept of tests*
> *aren't necessarily right. The tests*
> *are perfect but something could happen*
> *between the tests where it's good and*
> *then something happens where all of a*
> *sudden it's positive...*

My mom scoffs. "Yeah, it's called **getting sick.** Idiot."

"Okay but I feel like ragging on Trump isn't even fun anymore. Like it's just so mind-numbingly obvious it makes me want to vomit."

"I don't care, I have to call him out. I'm the fucking Resistance over here."

I laugh.

> So Mike knows about it and Mike has done what he has to. I think he's on an airplane, going to some far away place, but you'll be able to ask him later on...

"Matheus he isn't ready for this virus. Can you imagine? If he has to go through what I went through? It's gonna **annihilate** him."

"And it's only a matter of time at this point, right?"

"Oh yeah. It's totally closing in on him."

"When he gets corona, do you think he'll actually try all those bogus miracle cures? Or do you think he'll wake the fuck up and become Fauci's bitch?"

"I hope he sticks a UV light all the way up his ass and dies." She pops a jackfruit segment in her mouth and it squeaks between her molars.

May 10, 2020

Beep

My mom and I look up from our plates and furrow our brows.

"What is that?"

"Low battery on the smoke alarm?"

Beep

Didier lumbers into the kitchen, squinting, covering his ears. "What is that?"

My mom stands. "It's the smoke alarm, but it's just a low battery thing." She heads down the hall toward the noise and we follow.

"It's this one, right? The carbon monoxide?" She gives it a few tugs and it pops out of the wall.

"Mom you broke it!"

I punch Didier in the arm. "No she didn't, dumbass!"

"I didn't break it, Didier. Watch, it's gonna beep."

Beep

We follow her back into the kitchen where she pulls out a butcher knife and starts stabbing the back of that screaming little white box. Didier's face twists in agony.

"Mom I don't think you're supposed to be doing that! What if there's actually carbon monoxide?"

She pushes her hair out of her face and keeps at it with the knife. "It's not **beep beep beep**ing, Didier. It's just beeping."

He scowls. "So you're an expert on alarms? You know all the alarm sounds in the world and what they mean?"

Beep

"Idiot, everyone knows that's a fucking low battery sound."

"Don't talk to me, **faggot!**" He hustles outside like a little bitch and slams the back door. The batteries pop out.

"I think it's kind of bullshit that I get called a faggot in my own home. Like, as the parent in this situation, what are you planning on doing about that?"

My mom rummages through the junk drawer looking for new batteries. "I don't know what you want me to do."

"I want him to die."

"That's nice."

"I'm serious. I want him to die."

"Of all people, you should understand his anxiety issues."

"Didier doesn't have anxiety, he's just lazy and stupid."

She clicks the last battery in place, and the alarm begins to wail. "Fuck."

"Take it out! He's gonna freak!"

Didier pokes his head back in with his shirt collar pulled up over his nose. "I'm calling the police, you guys."

"No, look!" My mom holds up the batteryless alarm. "It's fine!"

"Are you sure?"

"Yeah, I just had to replace the batteries."

"Are you **sure** sure?"

"Yes! It's okay, I promise. Come inside, I just made food."

He grumbles something under his breath as he steps inside and slams the door behind him. "I'm going back to bed."

May 11, 2020

I pull up a seat at the little white table by the pool and I light a cigarette.

My mom looks up from her phone. "Can you help me with this Mother's Day caption? I'm totally stuck."

"Are you gonna post that selfie of us?"

"Yeah, here." She hands me her phone.

"Hm..." I zoom in on my face. "So what are we trying to communicate here?"

"I just want to make Nadia Donescu feel like shit about herself, you know?"

"Naturally."

"Like, look at me, I'm spending quarantine in Palm Springs with my fabulous gay son, and you're still stuck in Seattle with your fat husband. You silly cunt."

"Ugh, isn't she so bitter?"

"So bitter!"

"I hate her for that. But also I get it."

"Me too. She's a caged woman, she resents that I'm free."

I laugh and pass back her phone.

"Roll me a joint, will you? I need some inspiration for this caption."

I groan. "I'm so lazy! Can I do it after this cigarette?"

"Come on! It's Mother's Day!"

May 2019

"You have to try this. It's hummus made with **red bell pepper.**"
My dad smiles and nudges the tub of hummus toward my plate.

"Oh my gosh, Dad, you always have the fanciest stuff over
here."

"Ha!" He pats my back. "Then you should come see your old
man more often. I miss you, buddy."

"I know, I'm sorry." I stab a pita chip into the bell pepper
hummus. "It's been crazy this past month with Mom's house on
the market and everything. We're like, constantly cleaning."

"Mm." He grimaces as he watches me chew. "Do you like
the hummus?"

"Mm...mhmm. It's definitely bell pepper. Aren't you gonna
eat anything?"

"I ate before you came."

"Oh, okay."

"So tell me more about the move. Is your mother still planning on doing that...crazy road trip thing?"

"Yeah, she's gonna take a few months to drive down to
Austin, and then she's gonna decide where she wants to move

9

from there."

"So she's gonna sell her house and have nowhere to live?"

"Right. I mean, she'll stay at Airbnbs along the way."

"Mm. And you're going with her?"

"Yeah, I'm planning on meeting up with her somewhere in California after my short film wraps."

"So you're saying...you're leaving next month to do your film, and you're not coming back home?"

I frown. "I'm sorry, I thought you knew what was happening."

"You'd be surprised by how little I know. Your mother doesn't exactly keep me in the loop about these major life decisions."

"I'm really sorry about that. I'll tell her to stop being so annoying."

He chuckles softly. "It's fine, I don't want to cause any issues with her."

"That's probably smart."

"Yes."

I look down at my plate and fiddle with a pita chip. "So anyway. I, uh—I actually came over today because I wanted to talk to you about something. About my film."

"Okay."

"This is kind of difficult for me to say."

"It's okay, just say it."

"Well, we're still two thousand dollars short. And I was just wondering if there was any way you could help me out. Again."

He smiles politely and shifts in his seat. "Yeah, I don't know..."

"I get it, it's totally fine."

"What about your friends' parents? Are they not

helping out?"

"No, not really."

"Oh, man." He sighs and crosses his arms. "You know we've talked about this before, Matheus."

"I know."

"I'm happy to help you out when you decide to go back to school, but, these film projects with your friends..."

"No yeah, I get it. I'm sorry I asked."

May 13, 2020

"Oh my GOD what a fucking baby-dicked faggot! Cuck-ass soy boy beta fuck—BEHIND YOU BEHIND YOU! Jeffrey! Oh fuck—Jeffrey! HELP!!!!!! I'M GETTING MY ASS POUNDED! I'M SHOT!!!!!! I'M FUCKING SHOT!!!!!"

I turn over in bed and check my phone. It's 3am.

"Jeffrey, you're bad. You're really fucking shit at the game bro. Like, do you even want to get good? Or are you just fucking me up the ass with your baby dick?"

I cover my head with my pillow.

"WHAT? WHAT? Honestly dude you should just kill yourself. You should just take a big black cock in the eye socket and fucking kill yourself you faggot."

I fling off my sheets and storm into Didier's room.

"SHHHHH!"

"Jeffrey I have to be quiet now. Just don't yell over me, okay bro?"

May 14, 2020

"Did you hear Didier last night?" I pass my mom the joint.

"Mm, a little bit."

"It's kinda getting insane, isn't it?"

"I don't want to talk about Didier with you right now, you always take it in a negative direction. Can we just enjoy this high?"

"Fine."

"I just think it's something to keep an eye on. With fascism in vogue and whatnot."

"Your brother isn't a *fascist.*"

"Well yeah but that's a pretty low bar, don't you think? Imagine if you held him to the same standard you hold me."

"I don't hold either of you to any standard, Matheus. You're both useless shits."

"I'm sorry but there's no comparison between me and Didier. Like, he's literally a shitbag Nazi hermit."

"And what are you?"

"I have value to society, okay? I'm a fucking *artiste.*"

She laughs.

"I think you've just completely lost sight of how amazing

of a son I am because you're around me all the time. It's a shame, really."

"Is that what it is?"

"Yeah. I'm a fucking star."

August 2019

Meatlorfer glances at the monitor, then back at the candle-lit dinner scene. She takes a hit from her vape. ***"Sound!"***

"Sound speeds."

"Camera!"

"Frame."

"Scene two take two." ***Click***

"Good slate."

"Aaaand action!"

JUNE glides into the dining room and sets down a
lasagna at the center of the table.

                    JUNE
          Dinner is served! It's lasagna.

                  MR. KERN
        I can see that, dear. Looks great.

JUNE picks up a bottle of white wine and begins

pouring MR. KERN a glass. He grimaces.

                    MR. KERN
          Honey, I think lasagna goes better
              with <u>red</u>. Don't you think?

JUNE pauses, then lets loose a maniacal cackle.

                    JUNE
          Of course, dear! I'll take this one.

"Cut!"

Meatlorfer grabs my wrist and leads me around the camera equipment. We approach Mr. Kern at the head of the table.

"So..." She fans herself with the script. "I need you to be angrier."

"Angrier? Okay."

"Like an asshole dad, you know what I mean?"

"Sure."

"I know it's hard for you because you're gay and you're not naturally angry, but like, we need to dig a little deeper this time, okay?"

His face reddens and he chuckles a bit in disbelief. Around the room, crew members feign interest in their equipment, their headsets, their clipboards.

"Yeah I can do that."

"Was your dad an asshole?"

"Uh—no, not particularly."

"Well my dad's an idiot gorilla, so I know what I'm looking

for here." She slams her palm down on the table, rattling the dishes. "Like more of this energy, okay? Right, Matheus?"

"Mm...mhmm."

"Great, we're going for another take!"

—

"Did you see that last shot? At the dinner table?"

Leggy brushes her wigs and packs them into a briefcase. "Uh, sorta."

"What did you think?"

"I wasn't really paying attention, b. I'm sorry. I'm sure it was beautiful though."

"I think Meatlorfer's gonna ruin my movie."

"There's no way."

"She just keeps hammering at this angry dad thing and it's so one-dimensional. Like, zero nuance."

"So why don't you tell her that?"

"Are you kidding me? She doesn't give a fuck what I think. I mean she asks for my opinion all the time, but it means nothing."

"Damn."

"I'm just another one of her bitch boys, you know? It's so gross."

"Yeah, ew."

"And like, the blatant homophobia...it really jumps out on set, doesn't it?"

"Oh I know. That's honestly a big part of why we stopped being friends, cuz I felt so gross after Claire Cubed."

I shake my head. *__Fucking bisexuals...__*

Leggy snorts.

"I mean, I'm homophobic too, we're all homophobic, I love

to queer-bash as much as the next bitch. But like, on set, when she's in that position of power, it's just **gut-wrenching.**"

"Period."

"Fuck. Anyway." I wipe at my forehead. "I just needed to verbalize that."

"Anytime, b."

"I'm gonna go back out there."

"Okay. Good luck, bitch."

"Fuck me with a rake."

May 16, 2020

We hang on the lip of the pool and watch as a bee drags itself out of a wet splotch on the concrete.

"Do you think she'll be okay?"

My mom nudges it gently with a twig. "I think she'll be okay. She wasn't in the pool for very long."

"Is it just me, or are these bees throwing themselves in the pool on purpose at this point?"

"I know, right?"

"Like, what the actual fuck? Is *this* colony collapse?"

"I don't know." She takes a long drag from the joint. "That would be funny, though."

"Everyone's like, **save the bees,** but now I'm like, **do the bees actually want to be saved?** I think that's the real question moving forward."

"Cuz they're so ungrateful about it, aren't they? They just walk away like, **okay bye. Fuck you for intervening in my suicide.**"

"Exactly! They're just—"

Bang! The neighbor slams their back door.

"Shit." I put out the joint.

"Woah wait why'd you do that?"

"The neighbor!"

"That wasn't for us, Matheus."

"Yes it was."

"No it wasn't. And if it was, then fuck them."

"I feel bad. They're just trying to enjoy their backyard."

She clicks her tongue. "If they wanna come over here and talk to me like adults, that's fine. I'll talk to them. But if they're gonna slam doors, I don't give a shit."

May 17, 2020

I sit cross-legged in the grass and smoke a cigarette. Across the yard, my mom and Didier chat at the little white table by the pool.

I try to listen in on their conversation, but the sound of palm trees rustling in the breeze drowns them out. Occasionally she lets out a cackle that cuts through the white noise. I can't imagine what could possibly be so funny.

I put out my cigarette and cross the yard. As I approach them, Didier looks up at me and says something to her and they both break out in laughter.

"Hi, hello. Mom, I'm out of weed."

"Um...okay."

Didier stands and walks away. I take his seat.

"So, are *you* out of weed?"

"It's funny, Didier said you were coming to steal me away."

I scoff. "I'm not **stealing you away** from shit. You're a 50-year-old woman, you can decide who you want to talk to."

"Well you're always coming in and interrupting—"

"Are you out of weed?"

"I have enough for like two more days."

"Wow, that's great for you. Are you feeling generous?"

"No, not particularly."

"Are we really gonna do this little song and dance? Where I tell you I'm out of weed, and you're like, **tough shit,** and then I just end up smoking your weed anyway?"

"You need to talk to your father about raising your allowance."

"Yeah no, not happening."

"You could always get a job?"

"That's a good one, I have to write that down."

"Fuck off."

"Mom. Please. I'm getting uncomfortably sober."

"Fine! Get my AMEX."

"Yay! Thank you thank you!"

"Take out 200. I want four more things of Baby Jeeters, and you can spend the rest on flower."

"Perfect. I'll brb."

"Oh and Matheus, no indica please! For the love of god! You're always buying fucking indica!"

July 2019

"I was just wondering how much I could get for all this." I set my binder down on the counter.

"May I?"

"Yeah, go ahead."

He unzips the binder and begins flipping through the sheets of Pokémon cards. "How many cards are in here, approximately?"

"Like, 500."

"And what year were they purchased?"

"Uh, 2002 to 2008. Something like that."

"Do you know if any of them are shadowless?"

"I have no idea what that means, I'm sorry."

Leggy squeezes my arm and leans into my ear. *"I think the nerds are staring at us."*

"Stop." I suppress a smile.

Leggy steps up to the counter. "Hi, sir, is there somewhere we can wait while you do your appraisal thing for my friend?"

"Oh, I'll be done in a minute."

"Mkay." She widens her eyes at me. "So...can you believe...

Sally's little outburst last night?"

I smirk. "Oh, I know, I was so embarrassed for her."

"I mean, for her to show up at the bowling alley in the first place was just ridonkulous. No one invited her."

"No one invited her! That's why I pulled aside Danielle that one time. I was like, did you seriously invite this bitch?"

"I also pulled aside Danielle right as it was happening. She was absolutely gobsmacked."

"And she had every right to be."

"I mean I think we can all agree, when you put Sally in a bowling alley, shit will get toxic."

"And what about when she flicked that one girl's tit?" I start cracking up.

"Inexcusable! I mean that girl wasn't even involved. She was just sitting there minding her own business—"

He closes the binder. "I can't give you anything for this."

"What? Why?"

"Because you don't have any shadowless cards."

"I mean, nothing? Like not even 20 bucks?"

"Uh..." He scratches his head.

—

I hop in the car and hug my binder.

"Aw, b."

"What the actual fuck is a shadowless card? I'm so mad about that."

"I know. But at least you get to keep 'em, right? Maybe they'll be worth something in like, 40 years?"

"I don't give a fuck what they're worth in 40 years. I'm planning on being dead by 27, so, that's of no use to me." I roll down my window and light a cigarette.

 "How much do you still need to raise?"

 "Basically the full 2k, just to get this film off the ground."

 "Damn."

 "Yeah, shit's about to get pretty grim."

July 2019

Orange, California

Mr. Abner's House

Meet me in the pool house out back. Side gate is open xo

"Oh good, you're already here." He closes the door behind him.

I stand. "Hi."

"You can sit back down, son. Go ahead and get comfortable. Pop off your shoes."

I comply.

"Do you want anything to drink?" He opens a mini fridge. "Beer? Soda?"

"It's okay, I'm already plastered."

He chuckles. "Alrighty then. What about some iHeartRadio?"

"Uh, sure."

> *Head underwater but I'm breathing fine*
> *You're crazy and I'm out of my mind*

He takes a seat next to me on the couch and begins massaging my feet. "Is this good?"

"It's a little ticklish. I guess I'm just not used to it."

"Well you have very nice feet."

"Really? I always thought they looked kinda small and pudgy."

"No, they're great. Very sexy."

"Thanks..."

He pulls a wad of cash out of his pocket, counts out 300 dollars, and sets it down on the coffee table. "I don't play games, okay? I'm a pretty straight-forward guy."

"Of course."

"And if you need more, you just let me know and we can arrange something more. Alright?"

"Okay."

He slips off his cargo shorts and spreads his legs up on the couch. "Are you good? Are you comfortable?"

"Yeah, just do your thing."

He grabs my foot and brings it up to his crotch. I press gently into the base of his erect penis with my heel.

He leans back and groans.

May 20, 2020

Bang!

"Fuck." I put out my joint and shut my laptop. And then I close my eyes and sit still in the darkness while I wait for a scolding from the neighbors.

Nothing.

Bang!

Bang!

"The fuck...?" I stand up on my chair and peer into the neighbor's yard. All their lights are off, and their back door seems to be closed. And then, in that same slice of sky, a blue fireball shoots up in the distance and explodes into four fizzling streaks.

Bang! Like the sound of a door being slammed.

I cover my mouth in shock and watch as they keep coming in quick succession.

Bang!

Bang!

Bang!

Bang!

May 21, 2020

"It wasn't a normal firework, though. It was like a distress signal or something."

"What?" My mom stirs her white fish sauce at the stove.

"You know, like, the thing they shoot off of sinking boats."

"That doesn't make any sense."

"I know, right?"

"If someone needed help, why would they shoot a flare instead of just calling the cops?"

"I can't explain it either, but I know what I saw and I know it wasn't normal. Whoever shot that thing was not okay."

She struggles with a jar of capers. "Can you open this for me?"

I grab the jar and pop off the lid with ease.

"Thanks."

"It's kind of shocking how you're still this weak. Are you sure you're okay?"

"I'm fine, it's just my wrist. I think corona might've permanently fucked it up." She folds the capers into her sauce. "Will you also drain the rigatoni for me, please?"

I open the cupboard and pull out a colander. "Why aren't you more concerned about this distress signal?"

"I don't know, Matheus. Honestly, it sounds like one of your little stories."

December 2018

"Open." The doctor clicks on her flashlight and sticks a tongue depressor in my mouth. My mom watches over her shoulder.

"Say ah."

"Ahhhhh."

"You said it was the right tonsil?"

"Uhnnhuhnn."

She flips her light to the right, to the left, up, down. I can't imagine why. There's only one big bloody lump in my throat and it's pretty hard to miss.

My mom chimes in. "Do you think it's an infection?"

"No."

"Or maybe an abscess?"

"No, definitely not."

The doctor clicks off her flashlight and slides it back in her pocket. Then she feels for my lymph nodes under my jaw one last time.

"I didn't see anything."

I furrow my brows. "But you saw the growth, right?"

"I didn't see anything out of the ordinary." She peels off

her gloves and throws them in the trash. "There's some mild redness, inflammation, mucus. Which is all pretty standard for a smoker."

"Matheus also failed to mention that he had an amphetamine addiction in college."

"Mom I don't think that's relevant."

The doctor smiles wryly down at her clipboard. "I can refer you to an otolaryngologist if you want. But first I recommend you stop smoking for four days. And if you can still feel the lump, go ahead and make the appointment."

"What do you think it could be? Like, realistically?"

"I don't know, honestly. It could just be a stone lodged in there. Do you get tonsil stones?"

"Yeah, I've tried squeezing it before and a bunch of stones popped out, but, obviously I can still feel the lump."

"Tonsils are actually very delicate, especially at your age, so, I definitely wouldn't recommend pressing on them. Especially with your bare fingers. That actually might explain some of your symptoms."

"Oh. I mean, the lump was there before I touched it, so."

"Still, you need to stop. And stop smoking, too. Whatever this is, you aren't giving it a chance to heal."

—

"Do you think maybe she didn't see the full thing? It's much more menacing at an angle."

"No, I was watching. You could see everything."

"I don't know." I rest my head against the car window. "I think she seemed like kind of a crackpot doctor."

"Oh and the last doctor? Was he also an idiot?"

"Mom, you saw the thing on my tonsil. You asked her if it was an abscess, which means you saw it."

"I'm not a doctor, Matheus."

"It's just crazy to me how three different people can look at it and see **nothing**. It absolutely blows my mind."

"Okay, then we'll go to the otolaryngologist and figure it out. Easy."

"I don't even care anymore, honestly. I'd rather just die than have another doctor tell me I'm crazy."

July 2019

JUNE does the dishes at the kitchen sink. In the background, MR. KERN scrapes the rest of his lasagna into the trash.

                    MR. KERN
        Junebug, is this a pie in the trash?

                    JUNE
        Oh, yeah, it turned out terrible

                    MR. KERN
        Mm. Looks like Cynthia's lemon
                    meringue

JUNE clenches her jaw as she continues scrubbing the dishes.
ALTON enters frantically.

                    ALTON

Mom, I'm bleeding

JUNE
(over her shoulder)
What?

ALTON
I was brushing my teeth and I just
started bleeding

ALTON doesn't appear to be bleeding. JUNE breezes
past him and grabs a pack of cigarettes hidden in
the cupboard.

MR. KERN
June!

JUNE
No! You're not here all day! You don't
have to listen to every little thing
about his fucking teeth!

JUNE exits. ALTON tries to follow, but MR. KERN
grabs him by the arm.

MR. KERN
Do you see what you're doing to her?
You little shit!

"Here." Meatlorfer circles the script with a fat red sharpie. "I feel like this scene doesn't achieve its *dramatic potential.*"

"What does that mean?"

"Like, what if Alton was actually bleeding? What if he was presenting his mother with the baby teeth?"

I scoff. "That's so...literal."

"Okay I'm just trying to bring a cinematic perspective, you don't have to get offended."

"I'm not offended!"

"If the film's called *Baby Teeth,* the audience is gonna need to see a handful of bloody teeth at some point, are they not?"

"I feel like you still don't fully understand what I'm trying to do here, and it kind of terrifies me."

"Okay then explain it to me like I'm an idiot, because apparently I have no fucking idea how to access this hidden layer of meaning in your script—"

"Wait, you guys." Gina looks up from her laptop. "I just got an e-mail from an agent asking if his trans client can audition for Cynthia. What should I say?"

"Oh my god, of course. Does she have a reel?"

We all crowd around Gina's laptop. Leggy points at the screen and shrieks.

"Oh my god I know this bitch! She does drag! And she's like, semi-famous for being really drunk and messy on Instagram."

"Wait I love this."

Meatlorfer smirks. "Guys, don't make me say it."

"Oh come on!"

"I'm sorry but she looks like an old Frankenstein sex doll.

Cynthia's supposed to be **hot.**"

"I wanna give her an audition. I mean, this is a queer film, this is what it's all about."

"We would have to rewrite the character."

"No we wouldn't. That's the point."

Meatlorfer shakes her head furiously. "I'm not gonna cast an old drunk bitch as Cynthia and I don't think that makes me transphobic. Honestly, it's ridiculous that we're even wasting time on this conversation."

The cursor darts around Gina's screen. "What should I respond?"

"Do it. Send her the script."

May 24, 2020

Today President Trump threatened to withhold federal funding from the state of Michigan unless that state stops preparations to vote by mail in the upcoming election...

Didier walks into the living room with a carton of orange juice in his hand. "What the fuck are you guys watching?"

My mom looks over her shoulder. "It's our best friend Rachel Maddow! Yay Rachel!"

He scoffs.

It should be noted that this happened not only on a day when Michigan is dealing with one of the worst coronavirus death rates in this country, but also the day after a catastrophic flood in the central part of the state...

"Why is she so mad? It pisses me off so much when that bitch gets mad."

"Fuck off, Didier."

"Oh I'm sorry, are you offended because I attacked one of your favorite Democratic elite? Look who's in a cult of personality now!"

I look over at my mom in disbelief.

"Just ignore him, Matheus. He's joking."

"Hm." I sit back.

"Fucking fear-mongering horse-faced dyke."

"I—"

"Trump 2020! Wooooo!" He pumps his fist in the air as he heads down the hall. *"MAGA, MAGA, MAGA..."*

"Mom I don't think he's joking."

"He's clearly just trying to get a rise out of you."

"Do you think he talks like that in public?"

"Oh god no."

May 25, 2020

"After this episode, do you wanna walk the dogs with me?"

"Uh..." My mom looks up from her phone. "No, not really."

"Mkay. I just thought I'd ask, because you seem to be doing better lately, so."

"You know my wrist is still fucked up."

"Oh is it just the one wrist, or...both of them?"

She squints at me. "What are you trying to say?"

"I'm just saying, you seem to be doing better lately. And maybe it's time to start helping me out with the dogs again."

"Unbelievable. You know that's literally your only job around here, right?"

"Oop—not really. Cuz you haven't left the house since April, so, I'm pretty sure I've been running all the errands? Unless you're doing something behind the scenes that I'm missing?"

She wipes at her face. "I'm tired, Matheus."

"I'm tired too."

"Is it really that fucking difficult to walk two dogs?"

"Actually yeah, it is. Cuz Lily wants to stop and sniff everything and Kita just wants to run."

"Then don't take Lily. She's old, she doesn't even want to go."

"What an elegant solution. Mkay. Let's see how that plays out."

"Asshole."

I kneel down by the dog bed. "Kita, you wanna go for a walk?"

The dogs perk up.

"Oh, no, Lily, you're not going today. Yeah, Mommy decided she doesn't wanna take you."

My mom laughs. "Stop it, Matheus! Lily understands everything!"

"Oh I know, baby. Mommy says she doesn't love you anymore because you're old and fat. Yeah, I know. I don't think she gives a shit about me either."

"Fine! Goddamnit." My mom stands and brushes the crumbs off her lap. "I'm coming. Fuck you."

May 27, 2020

"Actually, no, my wrist is still fucked up from walking the dogs. Can you do it?" She hands me the garden shears.

I snort. "Okay. Anyway. Which one do you want?"

"Get this one, it's super pretty."

I snip off a fresh white rose. "This doesn't feel right."

"Why?"

"I don't know, doesn't it feel like we're killing the roses?"

"Manuel says it's good to cut them. Apparently they come back even better."

"Mm. Then shouldn't we cut all of them?"

"Uh..." She looks around and shrugs. "I don't know. I only needed a few."

—

I watch as she trims the rose stems over the kitchen sink.

"I think gardening might be my new quarantine thing. Wouldn't that be cute?"

"It's kinda gay."

"Huh. I thought you wanted a mom who does this sort of domestic crap."

"Yeah, maybe when I was like 9 and I needed that kind of energy in my life."

"Oh wow, apologies for the trauma."

"You know who I wish was my mom? Nadia Donescu."

"Nadia fucking Donescu! Yes, of course!"

"Isn't she great?"

"The best."

"She definitely would've kept me on the straight and narrow."

"Oh for sure. She's a natural disciplinarian. Firm, but gentle."

"That's exactly what I was just thinking, firm but gentle."

"And let's face it, children need that nuclear family structure. Without it, they just...pff." She motions toward me with her scissors.

"No I know, I'm definitely a cautionary tale. You know what we should be? We should be spokespeople for Josh Duggar's family values lobby. I can be like, ***my parents' divorce turned me into a gay crackhead prostitute.***"

"And I'll be like, ***I should've gardened more.***"

I laugh.

She drops the roses into a vase and holds it up. "Ta da!"

"That's actually gorgeous."

"Could Nadia Donescu do ***that?***"

"Honestly? Probably not."

May 28, 2020

"You know what I just remembered?"

My mom swims over to me. "What?"

"There's still no batteries in the carbon monoxide alarm."

She clicks her tongue.

"Am I supposed to just forget about that and move on with my life?"

"That's what I'm doing, and it's working beautifully."

"What if, this entire time, there's been a tiny little gas leak, and that's why we're all slowly going insane?"

"We're going insane because we've been in quarantine for two months. And we'd be dead by now if there was a gas leak."

I take a deep breath. ***"Shit."***

"What?"

"No, it's just—the air isn't hitting the bottom of my lungs."

"Matheus, I swear to god."

"No yeah at this point I'm locked into the death loop. It's just a matter of riding it out."

"Well if you could ride your death loop to yourself today, that would be great."

"You know what it is? I'm pretty it's that new sativa that's fucking me all the way up."

"Oh definitely."

"Have you also been getting way too high these last few days?"

"Sorta. But that's not really an issue for me."

"Yeah, I'm sorry, I need to get out." I wade through the pool. "The pressure underwater is like literally collapsing my lungs, and it's not the vibe right now."

"Don't do that! We were having such a nice swim!"

"I know, I'm sorry, I got way too high." I step out of the pool and wrap a towel around my shoulders.

"Where are you going? Back into the gas leak?"

"Yeah, it's fine. I'm sorry."

August 2019

"I think I'll just do half a tab. Right?"

Meatlorfer snorts. "What are you, an eight-year-old girl with leukemia?"

"I'm sorry, it's been a while for me! My tolerance is super low."

"Mkay, that's disappointing. I thought you were some kind of badass hardcore drug user, but I guess not? What about you, Gina?"

"Hold on—I'll do the full tab, fuck you."

—

Meatlorfer inspects a wall of polaroids in her bedroom. "Do you think I have too many pictures?"

"Uh..." I look up from my joint-rolling. "I always thought they were cool. But now that you mention it, it is a little intense."

"Right? It's like a thousand eyes watching me sleep." She rips a polaroid off the wall. "This is *John!* Why the fuck do I still have pictures of John?" She rips off a few more polaroids and shoves them in Gina's face. "Who the fuck are all these people, Gina? They mean *nothing* to me!"

Gina sits quietly up on Meatlorfer's bed and stares back at her wide-eyed.

"I think you're scaring her."

"Gina's gone mute! Why does nobody wanna talk to me on acid?"

"You're being too much right now. Come down here and help me roll more joints, it's fun."

"Fine." She sits down next to me in a huff and watches me roll. "I think that's enough, Matheus."

"What?"

"You've rolled enough joints, okay? Now it's time to talk."

"Talk about what?"

"Hey, look at me! Engage with me, please!"

"Dude I think we're just not on the same wavelength, you know? And that's fine, we can all do our own thing."

Meatlorfer scowls and turns away. And then everything falls silent except for the crinkling of my joint papers. My hands begin to tremble under the spotlight, and my fingers seize up, and the joint spills out all over the floor.

"Shit."

Meatlorfer breaks the silence. "Gina, it's time to come down here and contribute. You're too high above us."

Gina flashes a shaky smile and scoots over to the edge of the bed. We watch as she steps down slowly, cautiously, as if the bed were 10 feet off the ground. I hug my knees and sit back against the wall to make room for her, but it doesn't seem to be enough.

The moment her butt touches the floor, the ground cracks open and we free-fall down a mineshaft into the pits of hell. The light coming in through the window doesn't look like sunlight anymore, but like the orange glow from Earth's molten core. And the conversation outside between Meatlorfer's roommates becomes unintelligible demonic chanting. And then for a second it becomes extremely defined, and I can hear one of them say, **this is the highest I've ever been.**

Gina sets her hand down on my knee and it begins to grow roots.

                          GINA
        So I feel like we just got really low

                       MEATLORFER
                  Yeah, I felt it too

                          GINA
              Matheus are you okay?

                        MATHEUS
                 (without looking up)
          Yeah I'm fine. It's just a lot

                       MEATLORFER
              Why can't you look at me?

                          GINA
              Leave him alone, it's fine

                       MEATLORFER

```
I don't understand. I share acid with
my friends and then they ignore me


              GINA
Just try not to take it personally


           MEATLORFER
He said we weren't on the same wave-
length. What the fuck does that even
             mean?--
```

"I'm uncomfortable!"

Gina takes her hand off my knee, pulling the root out with it. At first she's taken aback, but then she beams. It's the most refreshing thing she's ever heard and all her pores are opening up to accept it. But I've just shattered something, and now I have to leave. I mutter an apology for nothing in particular as I scramble to my feet and head out the room.

I duck into a linen closet down the hall and pull out my phone. *Pick me up I'm dying lmao*

August 2019 (continued)

Santa Ana, California

Leggy's Car

The sky's gone nuclear sherbert.

We roll up to the stop sign at the end of Meatlorfer's street and Leggy flips on her right-turn signal.

Click.

Click.

Click.

It synchs with my heartbeat in a way that reminds me my heartbeats are finite.

I exhale. "Tell me something normal."

She leans over to check for oncoming traffic, and then we turn gently onto Almond Street. "Something normal?" The clicking stops.

"Yeah."

"Wait is this that anxiety exercise thing?"

"Just say anything. It helps to listen to a sober person."

"Uh—so I had a Caesar salad right after you left this morning. It was one of those pre-made ones in a bag that I love. And then like halfway through, I realized it was majorly expired. So that was a bummer."

I laugh, loudly. And she laughs too. Then suddenly I stop, because I've just shed another layer of reality and now laughter feels nauseatingly performative.

"You good, b?"

"No."

"What's wrong?"

"I'm just really high and really scared."

"Mm."

"I feel like I'm shedding a layer of reality every 30 seconds and I'm terrified of what's coming next, so, I'm sorry if I can't really talk right now."

"Oh, okay."

"*Fuck.* I'm sorry, everything I say on acid makes me sound like such an asshole."

"You're good, b. I'm just observing."

"Would music help?"

"Oh god, no."

"There's actually a lot I want to say to you right now, about what I'm experiencing and what happened at Meatlorfer's house. But it's not coming out, it's crazy. I feel like an idiot child with no vocabulary."

"I always feel like that on acid, too."

"And I'm sorry that everything coming out of my mouth right now sounds so fucking aggressive. *Shit!*"

She laughs. "You're not being aggressive at all. It's funny how you think that, though."

"I'm sorry. And I'm sorry for saying sorry so much. *Fuck!*"

"It's okay! Seriously, b—"

"I think it's better if you just stop interacting with me."

"Okay."

"Forget everything I've just said. It's all bullshit. What I've actually been trying to say this entire time is that I'm dying and I need help."

"What?"

"I have tonsil cancer."

"What the fuck?"

"It hasn't been confirmed by a doctor or anything like that. But there's this huge tumor in my throat and it's been there for almost a year and I can feel it pretty much constantly against the back of my tongue."

"Have you told anyone?"

"I told my mom. And we went to two doctors but they said it was nothing. I mean, they looked right at it and they said it was **nothing.**"

"Fuck." Leggy reaches out and grabs my hand. "That's so real."

The skin-to-skin contact overwhelms my senses, and suddenly I can't stop crying.

"Don't cry! You're gonna be okay, I promise."

"You mean so much to me."

"Aw, b. I know, so many emotions."

"Fucking shit." I wipe at my eyes. "I hate acid. What a terrible fucking drug."

May 29, 2020

"It's crazy how this whole thing blew up overnight." I pop an almond in my mouth as I scroll through Facebook.

"I know, right? It's like people are just dying to be part of something again."

"I don't know. I don't buy it."

"What do you mean?"

"Like, don't you think it's a little suspicious that every white person in America woke up a revolutionary this morning when George Floyd was murdered literally four days ago? I'm sorry, but how fucking fake is that?"

"So what? Better late than never."

"Mm. Are you gonna post something?"

"We probably should, right?"

"I'm not."

"Matheus! *Your silence makes you complicit!*"

"I don't know, it would be so cringe. Like I truly have nothing to add."

"Why? Are you not outraged?"

"Honestly, no. And neither are you. We can't even begin to understand outrage."

She clicks her tongue. "I'm a human being with a beating

heart, of course I'm gonna give a shit."

"But you didn't give a shit four days ago, right?"

"I did!"

"But not enough to post about it?"

"I don't know why you're getting so agitated with me, I'm not the bad guy here. You're the one who refuses to publicly condemn racism. That's very ugly, Matheus. Very, very ugly."

"Mkay."

July 2019

Gina opens the door and pops her head inside. "Cynthia's here."

Meatlorfer turns around. ***"The*** Cynthia?"

"Yeah. Are you guys ready for her?"

"Send her in, Gina, thank you." She widens her eyes at me. "Here we go..."

"Can you please make an effort to not be a total cunt right now? I know it's hard for you, but like, will you do it for me?"

"I'm just trying to do my job and cast the best fucking Cynthia in Orange County. Is that okay with you? Will you let me do my job?"

"I guess I'll just shut up then, because apparently my opinion on my own script means nothing."

"You haven't even seen her yet!"

"Exactly! And neither have you!—"

Gina opens the door. "Here's Shay."

"Hi everyone!"

"Hi, nice to meet you." I stand up and shake her hand.

Meatlorfer flips on her camera. "We're gonna be filming

your audition today, is that okay?"

"Oh, yes, I'm always ready for the camera."

"Will you say your full name and the role you're auditioning for into the camera please?"

"I'm Shay Cameron and I'm auditioning for the role of Cynthia Cripe."

"And you're not SAG, right?"

"No, darling, I'm not precious with my talent. I'm a multimedia entertaintress."

"Mkay. This is Matheus and he's gonna be reading you in. We're on page 5. Do you have any questions?"

"Uh..." She clutches her script. "I was just wondering, is Cynthia more of a sensual creature, or is she just one of those housewives with a stick up her ass?"

Meatlorfer looks over at me and raises a brow in amusement.

"What did you think, reading the script?"

"Well I don't know, but the only character I can really do is a sultry bitch like myself. I hope that's okay."

"Totally. You should just do it your way, and we could potentially build the character around you, so, don't worry about it."

"Alright, I'm just gonna go for it then."

"Okay, here we go." I clear my throat.

—

I light a cigarette on the porch steps and wave Meatlorfer away. "Fuck off."

"I didn't say anything!"

"You were smiling."

"I'm sorry but I think casting went really well and very I'm happy about it! Aren't you happy?"

"Dude...I can't believe she **sucked.**"

"I can. I knew it right away, as soon as I saw her picture. You should listen to me more often, you know? I'm the one with actual film experience here."

"It's just like—I wanted to cast hella queer people."

"You tried."

"And **everyone's white!**"

"You wrote a white story, so, that makes sense."

"No I didn't! What?"

"Yeah, the characters are clearly white. When other races try to read for it, it just sounds wrong."

"I'm gonna throw up."

"You're being too dramatic about this. Like, this isn't Hollywood. We're making a student film for four thousand dollars."

"No I know."

"Our lead actors are literally making a hundred bucks plus gas. Like, you aren't changing any lives here, you know what I mean?"

"Yeah."

"It's really not that serious."

May 30, 2020

And a little bit of chicken fried
Cold beer on a Friday night
A pair of jeans that fit just right
And the radio uuuuup

I step outside and find Didier sprawled out on a lawn chair.

My mom waves to me as she bobs around in the pool.

"Hey, Didier! You need to turn the music down!"

He gives me the finger.

"Mom! Tell Didier to turn it down!"

"What?"

"The fucking country music! It's way too loud!"

I thank God for my life
And for the stars and the stripes

"Matheus, everyone plays music outside!"

"There's a revolution going on in the streets! This is really fucking inappropriate!"

Didier turns down the music. "Can you guys stop fucking screaming?"

My mom turns to him. "Didier, can you please keep it at this volume? Your brother says there's a revolution in the streets."

"Sure, Mom. Thanks for asking like a normal person."

"No! Play something that isn't fucking nationalist or turn

it the fuck off!"

"Hey, *faggot,* go watch CNN."

"Hey, idiot, we watch MSNBC!"

"That's even worse. MSNBC's basically the Breitbart of you people."

I gasp. "Mom. No, Mom, please tell me you heard that."

"Matheus quit causing shit, for the love of god."

"Didier, tell her you're a Republican."

He laughs. "You're so pathetic, dude. It's hilarious."

"Are you a Republican, yes or no?"

"No, I'm not a Republican. But I'm also not a libtard like you. I like to think for myself."

I throw my arms in the air.

"And I'm not shitting my pants over Trump like you guys. You have no reason to hate him this much, nothing he does actually affects your lives."

"Did you hear that, Mom? Your son is a common idiot."

"He turned the music down, Matheus. Go back inside."

"For the record, Mom, I want you to know that you're just as retarded as Didier."

"Okay."

"That's all you have to say? *Okay?* Okay."

June 2020

June 1, 2020

"And two packs of Marlboro Lights 100's, please."

"ID?"

"Oh—yeah."

He picks up my ID and inspects it closely. "Washington D.C.?"

"Washington state. Like, Seattle."

"Mm. And date of birth?"

"Uh, October 27, 1997."

"Sir can you pull your mask down real quick?"

"Sure..." I pull down my mask and stare past him at the cigarette display.

"Mkay, go ahead and put your mask back on." He turns around and grabs two packs of cigarettes.

"Thanks." I slide my mom's AMEX into the card reader.

"Just so you know, I give all the cute boys a hard time."

"Oh wow." I smile reflexively under my mask. "Yikes."

"Don't tell me you're straight."

"God, no! I just wasn't expecting that today. I'm literally never expecting it."

"Welcome to Palm Springs, babe. Receipt?"

June 2, 2020

Bzzz. Bzzz. Bzzz.

"Are you gonna answer that, Matheus?"

"Um...no." I reach over and reject the call. "It's just Leggy trying to Facetime again."

"I thought you liked Leggy?"

"I do! I just hate Facetiming and she knows it."

"I think you should reach out. Invite her over."

"Really?"

"Of course! She's your best friend from college. It's ridiculous that we've been living in California for five months and I haven't met her yet."

"I don't know..."

"What, are you embarrassed of me?"

"Well yeah, a little bit. Mostly Didier. I just don't want to expose her to all this degeneracy."

She clicks her tongue. "If she's really your friend, she's not gonna judge us."

"Why are you pushing so hard for this? You don't even know her."

"I just think it would be nice if you had someone else to talk to. I'm tired of being the only member of your support system."

"Pff."

"Everyone needs friends outside the family, Matheus."

"Yeah, I don't need friends. Friends are for children and people who can't entertain themselves."

June 3, 2020

"JEFFREY HELP!! IDIOT! IDIOT! PLEASE DUDE OH MY GOD NOOOOO!!! AHHHHHHHHH!!!!" Didier throws his controller at the wall and unleashes a roar. *"FUCKING INBRED COCKSUCKING JEW!!!"*

Kita curls up next to me in bed and trembles as Didier rages on.

Bang!

I climb out of bed, cross the hall, and pound on his door. "Didier shut the fuck up!"

He stops for a second. And then he swings open the door and lunges at me.

"YOU SHUT THE FUCK UP MOTHERFUCKER!!!" He pushes me up against wall and punches me repeatedly in the stomach.

Bang!

Bang!

Bang!

I collapse on the ground gasping for air. He pins me down and starts punching the back of my head. *"LEARN! YOUR! FUCKING! PLACE! FAGGOT!"*

"Hey hey hey, stop it! Didier! STOP!" My mom tries to pull him off, but it's no use. Weak wrists.

Bang!

Bang!

Bang!

Bang!

I lift my head off the floor to find my mom sobbing next to me. Kita comes over and tries to lick my face.

"Where is he?"

June 4, 2020

My mom sets a glass of water down on my nightstand. "Are you feeling okay?"

"Mmhm."

"You wanna try eating something? I made a rasta pasta."

"No."

"Okay." She wrings her hands and looks around the room. "Is there anything else I can do for you?"

"It's just a fucking concussion, Mom. All I need is for you to shut up and stop bothering me."

"I'm so sorry."

"Wait, Mom."

"Yeah?"

"Can I smoke a cigarette in my room? The light outside hurts my brain."

"Yes!" She beams. "Yes of course! I'll go get your cigarettes."

June 6, 2020

I lie awake in bed and listen as my mom sobs into the phone.

"No, thank god he didn't press charges or anything like that. Can you imagine? ... I just can't. I can't keep doing this alone ... You don't understand. I tried, I'm always trying, but it's impossible ... You're not listening to me! Your boys are going to kill each other! It's not even—Oh! Oh yeah go ahead and blame me for everything. That's great, that really helps a lot ... Yeah, you too, right in the ass! Stupid bald bitch."

June 7, 2020

"A concussion kinda feels like being high. Except it's just the impairment part, and not the part where everything's trippy." I hit the joint.

My mom smiles sympathetically. "I'm glad you're feeling better today."

"Mm. I weirdly feel like I'm being rebooted."

"So, uh...I just wanted to let you know that I'm taking this whole situation very seriously."

"Oh, good."

"And I think it might be a good idea for you and your brother to separate for a while."

"Right."

"So I talked to your father, and we decided to send one of you up to Washington for a few weeks."

"Well it sure as shit isn't me, right?"

"Didier doesn't want to go either."

"Tough shit. The aggressor gets the punishment, period."

"Matheus—"

"This shit is bananas, b-a-n-a-n-a-s. This shit is bananas! B-a-n-a-n-a-s!"

"And what about for me? Is this shit not bananas for me, too?"

"Honestly, hoe..." I chuckle. "I'm so over it. Nothing can surprise me anymore, nothing can hurt me anymore. Do your worst."

"I'm not trying to hurt you."

"Do you know what Didier said to me as he was beating me unconscious? He said, **learn your fucking place.** Faggot. And you know what my place is? This, right now, the thing you're asking me to do. I'm the one who has to suck it up and take one in the ass, always, in everything. And I honestly don't care anymore, cuz I just dropped like 15 IQ points and it feels really fucking fantastic. So yeah, please, do your worst. Go ahead and make your worst possible decision as a parent."

"Mm." She hits the joint and looks out over the pool. "I think you're glossing over your own culpability in all this."

"**My** culpability?"

"The way you belittle Didier."

"Please!"

"You've been calling him an idiot his entire life. What do you think that does to a person?"

"Didier **is** an idiot, and I think he should know it."

"He's my son! And **I'm** the parent! I'm still the fucking adult here, goddamnit!"

"Mhmm, you're doing a great job sweetie."

"That right there is your problem, Matheus. You're a bully and a bitch and you think you know more than everyone else."

"Okay, cool. Are you gonna fight me too?"

She scoots back forcefully in her chair and walks off with the joint.

August 2019

"Alton, show me your best gay face." Meatlorfer watches the monitor.

"Should I—should I try it with the cigarette?"

"Yes! Goddamnit, who keeps moving Alton's clove cigarettes? *Gina!*"

"Sorry sorry sorry, I'm right here." Gina pats her pockets and produces the pack of clove cigarettes.

"For the love of god, Gina, will you go splash some cold water in your face? I feel like I'm being assaulted by your crusty little eyes right now. Alton, are you ready?"

"Uh..." Alton looks down at his script. "I'm still not entirely sure what you want me to do."

Meatlorfer sighs. "It's really simple. You're eavesdropping on your mother's coffee date with Cynthia, and you're twirling around the cigarette you stole, and you're just feeling very gay and sassy about it."

"Okay. I just—I still don't really know what you want me to do with my face."

"Just—look at Matheus. Matheus, do the gay face."

70

I let out a nervous cackle and cover my mouth. "I'm sorry. I'm really sorry, I'm not laughing at you. I'm just like...what?"

"Okay, everyone take five!" She grabs my wrist. "You're coming with me."

"What you just pulled in there was way out of line." She lights a cigarette.

"I'm sorry, I just thought I could—"

"Laughing in my actor's face! And right before an extremely vulnerable shot!"

"I wasn't laughing at him, I was laughing at the situation. Cuz suddenly 15 people were looking at me and expecting me to do something gay with my face and I was just like...where even is this in the script?"

"Okay, let me explain to you how set works. You come here, you listen to your superiors, you follow your orders **blindly,** okay? This isn't about making you feel comfortable, it's about getting the fucking shot. I'm the director for a reason, right? Because I know things that you don't? Would you agree with that?"

"Yeah."

"Cool, so, I'd like you to stop undermining me in front of my crew. I know you've been talking shit about me behind my back, okay? Gina tells me everything. That has to stop."

My stomach drops.

"What you don't seem to understand is that I have to be two times louder and two times cuntier than any male director just to get those fuckers to take me seriously. Every damn day I come in here and I have to prove myself to them all over again. I don't need you running around here trying to tear me down, cuz everyone's already doing that. Are you following?"

"No yeah, I'm—I'm really sorry."

"If I ask you to do a gay face on my set, you shut the fuck up and do a gay face. It's really that simple."

"Copy."

"Now do it. Do the gay face."

I purse my lips a bit.

"That's it! Was that so fucking hard? Wait, hold it exactly like that, let's go back inside."

July 2019

Gina smiles and hands the receptionist a flyer. "Hi there!"

"Hi."

"I'm Gina and this is Matheus. We're with a group of film students from Chapman University, and we're interested in shooting a scene in your waiting room for our upcoming film. It'll be on the morning of August 18th, which is a Sunday. All the info's right there on the flyer."

The receptionist studies the flyer. "Oh wow, okay."

"Yeah, and if any of you guys are interested, we still need a few extras. Receptionists, dental hygienists, whatever."

"Forreal? Like no auditions or anything?"

"Nope! I mean, you probably wouldn't have any lines. Maybe one line?" Gina turns to me. "Right?"

"Yeah there's one receptionist line. But it's hot."

The receptionist beams. "That's actually really cool. I'll make sure to hand this to my office manager when she comes back."

"Great! Tell her we're open to negotiations, and to contact me with any questions or concerns. That's my number and my e-mail right there at the top."

"I will do that!"

"Thank you so much! Have a good one."

"Bye!"

—

I hop in the car and buckle my seatbelt as Gina types the next location into her phone.

"I can do the next one, if you want. You shouldn't have to do all of them."

She snaps her phone into the stand and presses go. "It's totally fine. I don't mind talking to people."

"That one went pretty well, don't you think?"

"There was no ceiling fan."

"What?"

"Ceiling fan, teetering on its axis. Isn't that the first line of the script?"

"Oh shit, you're right."

"It's not a big deal, we're not in a position to be choosy right now. And we could always just do a close-up of a random ceiling fan that kinda matches the room. It'll be fine."

I smile and study her face as she slips on her sunglasses. "Gina, honestly, you're kind of a boss bitch. Like I'm just now realizing your power."

She laughs.

"No I'm serious. Like you're actually out here on the ground floor getting shit done, all while getting punched in the cunt constantly. I could never be a producer. I don't know how you do it."

"Thank you for saying that. I appreciate it."

"Well I don't think it gets said enough."

"I mean, out in the real world, producing isn't like this at all. But yeah, producing a student film is a lot of grunt work."

"Right."

"And technically in a low-budget situation like this, the director is supposed to be helping out, but like..."

"Meatlorfer."

"Exactly."

"Okay Gina, real talk, why do you stick with Meatlorfer? Like we're all dying to know what you get out of this dynamic."

"I know." She sighs. "I don't know...it's complicated. Why do *you* stick around?"

"Gina that is some fucking piping hot tea that you just spilt in my lap you raging psychopath."

"See? It's complicated."

"But it shouldn't be complicated, right? Like if someone's abusive, that should always be a hard line."

"It's just—it's not **all bad,** okay?"

"Really bitch? Like what?"

"I don't know, like...it actually feels pretty good to know that she trusts me with all this work. It's a sign of respect, in her own fucked up way."

"That's a hot take on exploitation."

"Yeah it's funny, cuz it might look like Meatlorfer's walking all over me, but the truth is that I've never had more power under any other director. It's like we have an unspoken understanding. She bullies me in front of the crew to look big and bad, but at the end of the day, she's not all up in my business about how I do my job. It kinda works."

"That's interesting."

"I mean obviously it doesn't always work, because here I am teaching my writer how to location scout, but like..."

"No yeah I know exactly what you mean. I think I'm also one of those people who thrives under neglect. It's kinda like what I have with my mom."

"Mm."

"Like, she's never really been a *mom* mom. It's more like, my real mom died in a fire and then my crackhead prostitute aunt who's only five years older than me got custody. Which sounds like a bad time, but like...I'm fucking living. She lets me do whatever the fuck I want, since I was like 8 years old. And honestly, I'm grateful for that, because it gave me the space to find out who I was and what I liked to do from a really early age. I probably wouldn't be an artist today if my mom had given a shit about me."

June 8, 2020

"Knock knock!" My mom stands in my doorway and holds up a white paper bag. "Special delivery!"

"What is that?"

"Just a little something I picked up for you at the dispo." She sits down on the edge of my bed and hands me the bag.

"What is this? What are you doing?" I open the bag to find a bundle of keef-crusted blunts.

"It's apology weed. I'm trying to apologize."

"Oh shit." I sit up in bed. "Go on."

"I've been thinking a lot about what you said yesterday. And you're right, Didier has to be the one to go. So I talked to him, and I talked to your father, and we all agreed that this is what's best for now. We booked him a flight and everything. He leaves this weekend."

"Oh, okay. I don't really give a shit."

"I thought you'd be happy..."

"Do you want a fucking gold medal for doing the bare minimum as a parent?"

"I just want us to be good again. I miss you." She tries to touch me and I brush her off.

"I'm not in the mood to give you the reaction you're

looking for."

"I know." She stands. "I just wanted to say sorry."

"Mhmm."

"Oh, and I was just thinking—feel free to say no, but do you want to go out to lunch tomorrow? Or whenever? We can finally try that ridiculous taco place on Palm Canyon."

"It's open?"

"Yeah, I think everything's back open."

"Holy shit, when did *that* happen?"

"I know, right?"

"Sure, yeah, I'm down."

June 9, 2020

"Can I get you guys started with any drinks?"

My mom points at her big plastic menu. "Can I get a loco caliente prickly pear margarita?"

"And can I just get a Sprite, please?"

"For sure! One loco caliente prickly pear margarita and one Sprite."

"Thank you."

The waitress walks away and my mom leans in across the table. *"I thought we were both ordering ridiculous margaritas!"*

"I know, I'm sorry, I chickened out at the last second."

"I can order something for you if you want?"

"No, seriously, it's fine. I'm already having a blast."

"Me too." She reaches out and grabs my hand. "Thanks for coming out with me."

"Thanks for paying, bitch."

The door swings open. A wide-eyed family enters the restaurant and idles awkwardly by the empty podium.

"You know what's tripping me out?"

"What?" She sets aside her menu.

"When you walk inside, you're supposed to be wearing a mask, right? Like it says so on the door, *no mask no service.*

But then when you sit down, you're allowed to take it off? How does that make any sense?"

"Well, you can't eat with a mask on."

"I mean yeah, but what good is the mask at the door if we're all just gonna be maskless in a closed room together anyway?"

"I don't know, and honestly I don't care. We have antibodies."

"Still, it's a glaring contradiction."

"You know what would be super useful? Little ID badges for people who've developed antibodies. That way we wouldn't have to wear a mask in public."

"A little ID badge, like, the Star of David?"

"No!" She laughs. "Not like the fucking Star of David. Like a little green check mark or something."

"No yeah, that's way too dystopic for me."

Our waitress emerges from the kitchen with my Sprite. The family at the podium watches as she breezes past them.

June 10, 2020

"Oh wow, look at that moon!" My mom sits up in her lawn chair and points her phone up at the sky.

"Mom, I swear to god, if you post one more picture of the moon, I'm calling the police and shutting down your Instagram."

"Am I allowed to just have it on my camera roll? For me?"

"I mean yeah, as long as you know you're a terrible photographer and pictures of the moon are stupid."

"Matheus, I don't expect you to understand my passion for the stars."

I laugh.

"You with your narrow, terrestrial-bound mind."

"Right."

"My mind, it operates on a much grander scale. Physics, *astro*physics. Numbers, concepts. Things you wouldn't be able to grasp—"

Bang! A flash of blue light. And in the sky, four fizzling streaks.

I look over at my mom as she covers her mouth in shock.

"I told you, bitch."

"Holy fuck."

"There it is. The distress signal. Isn't it distressing?"

"No, Matheus, that was a *ghetto firework.*"

I laugh. *"A what?"*

"You've probably never seen one before. It's like, cheap explosives."

"What does it mean?"

"I don't know. Maybe gang related? Like some sort of cop warning system?"

"In *Palm Springs?*"

"You never know."

"Here's what I don't understand: why haven't their neighbors complained about the noise yet? Like, imagine being right under that thing every night! It just doesn't make sense. I'm telling you, Mom, there's something going on here and I think multiple people are involved."

"Should we call the police?"

"I don't know. That would feel so wrong."

"There's a reason this shit's illegal here, you know? It could start a fire."

"Then what should we do?"

"You know what?" She grabs her phone. "I'll make a post about it on Nextdoor, and then it's not our problem anymore. How about that?"

June 11, 2020

"We got several hits on Nextdoor. About the fireworks."

"Oooh!" I take a seat next to her on the couch. "Show me!"

"There's a lot of useless bullshit, so I'm just gonna read you the gems."

"Oh my god, okay."

"Okay, so...here's one. Sondra Hill says she's been hearing fireworks too. But then she goes off on a tirade about military spy planes, so, I'm not sure her testimony would hold up in court."

"I'm Sondra Hill."

"Wait, this one's my favorite: Henry Whitmore says ear plugs are just 99 cents."

"Burn, Henry Whitmore, burn."

"And then basically every other comment just says they haven't heard it."

"Wow. This is what it feels like to be crazy, by the way. Isn't it so unsatisfying?"

"You know what, Matheus? I think our friend Henry might have a point. Like, how much are these fireworks really affecting our lives? Almost not at all."

"Okay I'm sorry, but I'm not like you or Henry Whitmore, I

can't just ignore this major unexplained event in the sky going on every night."

"You need a hobby, Matheus, seriously."

"I'm fully prepared to die on this hill. There's something sinister going on with those fireworks."

"Maybe it's time to call Dr. Chinn."

"Shut the fuck up."

"She's probably doing sessions over Zoom. I think it might be good for you to get back on antidepressants."

"I don't need antidepressants, I need fucking Xanax and Adderall and mood stabilizers, but everyone's too pussy to prescribe it to me, so, it's all just a huge fucking waste of time."

"It's not like everyone with anxiety is just walking around suffering 24/7. There are solutions, Matheus. I think maybe you just don't want to get better."

"Is that what it is?"

"You're a victim, you love to suffer. You get that from your father."

August 2019

"You ready, b?"

"Wait, no." I cover my mouth. "I'm scared you'll think it's gross and have a bad reaction."

"I won't!"

"Promise me you won't look shocked in the face? Like no matter how mangled and bloody it is?"

"I promise."

"Shit, okay."

I open my mouth and Leggy shines her phone flashlight inside.

"Oh, okay. Yeah."

I close my mouth. "Did you see it?"

"I saw ***something.*** Not as bad as you described, but, yeah. Your tonsil's a little wonky-doo."

"You saw the big bloody lump on my right tonsil?"

"Clear as day, bitch. I have no idea what your doctor was on."

I laugh. "Oh my god. You can see it!"

"Is that a good thing?"

"Yes!" I beam. "It means I'm not clinically insane!"

"And now what?"

"What do you mean?"

"Like, what are you gonna do about your tonsil?"

"Oh, I'm thinking of just letting it kill me slowly."

"Oof."

"What do you think? Good idea? Bad idea?"

"Bad idea, definitely."

"Hm."

"I think you should make an appointment with a specialist, b."

"See, I thought about that. And then I thought about that moment when the doctor comes in and sits down with me and my mom and tells us that I have cancer. And I don't think I can handle that. I don't think I ever want to know *for sure* for sure what it is, cuz I already know it's really bad. But it'd still be nice to have some informal validation that like, yeah, it's real. Yeah, you've got a fucking lump in your throat and you smoke like a chimney, so, shit."

"Shit."

"Exactly."

"So you want people to treat you like you're sick, but you don't want to go to the doctor, and you're expecting all your family and friends to just sit back and accept whatever happens?"

"In an ideal world, yeah."

"That's fucking hilarious."

June 12, 2020

"And can I get two packs of Marlboro—"

"Yeah yeah." He grabs my cigarettes and rings them up.

"Thanks."

"You know if you sign up for a 7-Eleven rewards membership, you get a dollar off every time you buy two packs? It really adds up."

"Oh shit, I had no idea."

"Yeah, just go ahead and type in your number for me please."

"Wow, thanks for hooking me up."

"No problem! Gotta keep my favorite customer coming back, right?"

I snort. *"I'm* your favorite customer?"

"Yeah, why not?"

"That's kinda sad for you."

"What? No way! You're like the best part of my day!"

"Jesus...do you talk to all the twinks like this?"

"Babe, I hate to break it to you, but you're not a twink. You're like a full-grown otter."

"That's...literally the nicest thing anyone's ever said to me."

June 13, 2020

I wake up at 5am to the sound of rolling luggage.

"Is that all you're bringing?"

"Yeah, just clothes and shit. I'm gonna leave the rest here for when I come back."

"Okay. What about your video game things?"

"It's all online. Can we go?"

"Wait, do you have a mask?"

"No."

"You don't have a mask?"

"No!"

"Shit, okay. I think I still have my old one in the junk drawer. You have to keep it on the entire flight, okay?"

"Okay! Let's go!"

June 14, 2020

My mom rips the fitted sheet off Didier's bed. "Oh my god."

"Holy shit, what is that?"

"I think it's just a sweat stain."

"Just a sweat stain?"

"Here." She wrinkles her nose and drops the sheets into a hamper. "Can you go wash this? Immediately?"

"It's like he was growing into the bed."

—

I turn on the washer. *"Hey mom!"*

"What!"

"Should I get the pet spray for the mattress!"

"No! Get the vinegar!"

—

We sit on opposite ends of Didier's mattress and scrub at the sweat stain with vinegar-soaked rags.

"Now that Didier's gone, I'm gonna need you to call me a faggot at least twice a day to keep my ego in check."

"I'm not gonna do that, Matheus."

"Fine, then my ego is just gonna pop off totally unchecked and you're not gonna like it."

"Faggot."

"No, you gotta grit your teeth a little. Like you're genuinely pissed off that I'm allowed to call myself a human being."

"Faggot."

"Oh, that was good! Yeah, I definitely felt that one."

June 15, 2020

My mom shoots up out of the water, rips off her snorkel, and adds another cigarette butt to a wet little pile on the concrete.

"Are you gonna help me clean the pool are you just gonna sit there smoking like an asshole?"

"I'm bored."

"Great, then grab a snorkel and jump in!"

"No, like, I'm **fundamentally** bored. With life."

"Jesus Christ." She climbs out of the pool and wraps a towel around her shoulders.

"Let's go to LA. Let's go to a protest and get arrested."

"No thank you."

"D'you know they're saying that BLM is officially the biggest social movement in America since the civil rights era?"

"So?"

"So, it's the biggest fucking movement in 60 years and we didn't even slightly participate. It just completely passed us by and we're still the exact same people we were before. Isn't that crazy?"

"I thought you said we didn't have the right to be outraged?"

"You can't listen to me though, I'm full of shit."

She pulls up a seat at the little white table and lights a

half-smoked joint.

"I think maybe Didier was right about me being a liberal idiot."

She laughs. "If you're an idiot for hating Trump, then I'm an idiot. And I'm not an idiot."

"It's not even about hating Trump, it's just like—what the fuck am I doing? I'm doing nothing. I'm learning nothing. I haven't read a book in like two years. I think I might be a really shitty artist."

"Your writing is fine, Matheus."

"It's bullshit. I have nothing to say."

"You're 22 years old, what could you possibly have to say?"

July 2019

I tie my shoes as Mr. Abner counts out the cash.

"Hey, do you maybe want to stick around for a bit?"

I look up at him and smile. "Sure!"

"I just—I picked up some pot." He reaches into his robe pocket and pulls out a little glass jar full of joints. "I'll throw in another 100 bucks if you stay and smoke with me?"

"Oh my god, I'm not gonna charge you to smoke me out!"

"Are you sure?"

"Yes, I'll gladly be here for free."

"Okay, cool." He sparks a joint and passes it to me. "I usually don't do this. I just find it incredibly easy to talk to you. You don't know how rare that is for your age group."

"No I know."

"Most of these kids, they don't seem to understand that this is also about companionship."

"Right. I mean that's something I get out of this, too. The companionship."

"Really?"

"Yeah, and it doesn't hurt that you're a total dilf."

He laughs.

"I'm serious. You're not like other guys who pay for sex."

"And why's that?"

"Because you're sexy and normal and not at all desperate."

"I don't **always** pay for sex. I date occasionally, women. This is just how I like to do things with men."

"Mm."

"I guess technically I'm bi, I just never properly came out. Never felt like I **had** to, you know?"

I squint at him and nod.

"I don't know. That's enough about me. Tell me about you."

"Uh...what do you want to know?"

"Tell me about your film. What is it about?"

"Oh, god. It's uh—it's not really about anything."

He laughs. "Seriously?"

"It's hard to give a synopsis because it's pretty weak on plot. I've always been shit at plot. But basically it's about a gay kid who's scared of his teeth falling out."

"Oh, interesting."

"It's actually not. It's shit. The director—she's toxic. Totally stifles my creative energy. I hate everything I'm writing right now."

"I wouldn't be so hard on myself. I mean clearly you're a bright kid with a lot to say."

"Yeah, I heard that a lot growing up. Maybe too much, actually."

"Mm."

"People used to tell me I was mature for my age cuz I didn't like monkeying around with the other boys, but I was actually just a flaming homosexual. And they used to tell me I was smart, but honestly I only cared about grades so much cuz I desperately needed validation from somewhere. And now that I'm getting older, I'm starting to realize I might just be...average? Or maybe even slightly below average? Just an average-ish white gay man."

"Would that be so bad?"

"Oh it would just be the worst."

August 2019

I pace around the kitchen island rummaging through drawers with a bottle of wine in my hand.

The girl at the stove turns around. "Can I help you find something?"

"I'm just looking for a corkscrew. I have to empty this out and fill it with grape juice for the dinner scene."

"Ah." She opens a drawer by the stove and produces a corkscrew. "It's kinda dumb how they keep it over here with the cooking stuff."

"Thank you so much! I'm Matheus, by the way."

"Itziana. Crafty." She steps aside and motions toward a baking pan full of unsauced enchiladas.

"Damn, you're really going for it." I stab the corkscrew into the bottle and twist.

"I know crafty usually means picking up Cane's and stacking granola bars, but I legitimately enjoy sharing my food with people. How lame is that?"

"I think taking pride in your work is literally never lame."

"What do you do here?"

"I'm the writer. So basically my job on set is to get in every-one's way." The cork pops out.

"You can come bother me whenever! No one ever fucking talks to me on set."

I grab two plastic cups and start filling them with wine. "Itziana, please feel free to say no, but do you wanna kill this bottle with me as quickly as possible before Meatlorfer finds out?"

"Oh my god, fuck yes." She whacks her spoon clean against the rim of the pot and picks up a cup.

"Cheers. By the way, I'm not an alcoholic. This is just me reaching a very natural breaking point."

"Same."

We chug.

"Fuck." I set down my cup and grimace. "I feel like wine shouldn't be the hardest alcohol to chug, but it is."

"I know, right? What's up with that?"

"Blech." I tilt back my cup and finish it off with one more dreadful chug. *"Descosteng."*

"Are you good?"

I pour myself another. "I don't know. Yes? Or at least I will be very soon. My movie's kinda shit if you haven't noticed, Itziana."

"Oh..."

"This is the part where you're supposed to say, *no, it's great! You're great! Everything's great!"*

"Bro, I'm so sorry, I honestly haven't been paying that much attention! I'm on my phone all day playing some stupid cross-word shit."

"That's actually so fucking refreshing, you have no idea."

Gina bursts into the kitchen. "Matheus, where's your headset?"

"I never got one. Was I supposed to have a headset?"

She looks down at my cup. *"Shit,* okay. Meatlorfer wants you to keep the actors company in the dressing room while we set up for the next shot."

"Oh, okay, I was just doing the wine."

"I'm pretty sure nobody asked you to do that."

"No yeah, I just thought I'd get a head start on it—"

"Okay, off you go. Go go go."

"I'm going!"

—

"This casting director the other day, she was like, you're not old enough to play a mom. And I was like, lady, I'm literally playing a mom to a *teenager* in a student film right now. And then she laughed right in my face! She said there was no way, I had to be lying."

I smile weakly. "Oh my god, that's craaaazy."

"I don't look *that* young, do I? You can be honest with me."

"I think it'll all...be okay...in the end."

She snorts. "Are you on something right now?—OW!"

Leggy pulls back her flatiron. "Sorry girl! Are you okay?"

"Yes just please be more careful!"

"I'm so sorry."

June touches my forearm. "Well anyway, what was I saying? Whatever, it's gone now. Hey, do you know when Cynthia gets here? I wanna have enough time to build a rapport with her before our scene."

"I actually don't know, but I can text Gina and ask."

"You don't know Cynthia's call time? You don't have the sheet or whatever?"

"No." I laugh. "I'm just the writer, they didn't even give me a headset. Can you believe?"

"Wow..."

Leggy unplugs the flatiron and sets it down on the counter. "Hey, Matheus, do you remember where you packed June's earrings this morning?"

"Um...no, I don't."

"Can you come to the bathroom and help me look?"

"Yeah, for sure."

Leggy shuts the door behind us. *"I figured you might need a break from that hoe."*

"She literally insulted me like three times in the span of 20 seconds."

"And what about that rant on the perils of method acting?"

I snicker. *"Stop! She's gonna hear us."*

"Are you actually drunk, b?"

"Yeah! I chugged the dinner wine with that bitch on crafty."

"That's fucking hilarious."

"Okay wait, where are the earrings?"

"There's no earrings. She's literally fucking wearing the earrings as we speak."

"Oh my god, you're terrible."

"Here, open some bags so it sounds like we're looking."

June 18, 2020

"Mom what are you doing smiling at your phone? Who are you talking to?"

"No one!"

"Come on, I know you're talking to someone."

"Can I just have one thing in my life that you don't know about?"

"So it *is* a man!"

"Yes, it's a man."

"Is it someone I know?"

"No, it's just—it's a guy I went to high school with. Random guy, not from my friend group."

"Stranger danger! What's his name?"

"I'm not telling you his name, you're just gonna look him up."

"Well yeah, no shit."

"I wanna keep this private Matheus, please. You always ruin the fun for me with your criticisms."

"Is he fat? Is that what this is about?"

"No, he's not fat!"

"He sounds fat. But whatever, I'll respect your privacy."

"Thank you."

"You know I also have something of a new flame myself."

"Oh really, who?"

"This cashier at 7-Eleven."

"Shut up."

"I'm serious. He openly flirts with me and tells me I'm his favorite customer."

"Is he hot?"

"Not really. You know I have this disease where I'm only attracted to straight guys."

"Still? I thought that was just a phase."

"Unfortunately, no, it's looking like a permanent fixture of my sexuality."

"Mm. That is unfortunate. You should work on that."

August 2019

Santa Ana, California

Leggy's Apartment

I sit cross-legged on the rim of Leggy's bathtub wearing a plaid miniskirt we found at Goodwill. Leggy sits on the toilet and sifts through her makeup bag.

"Look up." She uncaps a mascara wand and brings it up to my face.

"Can you make it extra clumpy, please? I wanna look like British white trash."

"Of course, b."

"Thanks."

"God, your bottom lashes are to die for. Do you know how insanely rare that is?"

"No I know. Sometimes I see bitches with literally nothing on their bottom lid, and I'm just like, are you okay? Is there not constantly debris in your eye?"

"Oh my god, stop moving."

"Sorry, lol."

"And...done!" She sits back and beams. "Oh my god babe, you look so good already!"

"Can I see?"

"Wait, no, just one more thing." She pulls out a tube of red lipstick.

"I don't want lipstick, it makes me look really masc and severe."

"I was just gonna use it on your cheeks, if that's okay?"

"Oooh, yeah. Go for it."

She dabs the lipstick on my cheekbones and taps it out with her finger. "It's a little blotchy, but like, that's the vibe. It's editorial."

—

I turn my face over in the mirror, and then I step back and take in the whole look. "I. Am. **Woman.**"

"How do you feel, b?"

"I feel like...a rich Persian man's dirty little secret."

She laughs. "Does it turn you on?"

"No, but I get the appeal. Dressing up."

"Right?"

"Here, can you take a pic?" I hand her my phone and I strike a pose against the bathroom counter.

"Okay wait, try one hand on the wall—no like—okay now your balls are out. Yeah, like that! Oh bitch yes!"

"What about with a cigarette?"

"Oh my god, yes, that looks so hot. Girl, that's a Tinder profile for sure."

"Lemme see." I grab my phone and smile down at the screen.

"It's actually really frustrating how fuckable you are as either gender."

"Ew, stop!"

"I'm serious, you should go to set like this tomorrow. I bet you could give **Walter** a **boner.**"

My smile fades. "You're making fun of me."

"What! No I'm not!"

"He's obviously straight, it's not like I can **give him a boner.**"

"You don't know that!"

"Yes, I do."

"He could be bi."

"Rule 1: don't bank on bi. Next topic."

"Damn, I thought you liked him..."

"I mean yeah, I like his face. And I like to imagine him taking a hands-free piss at a stadium urinal. But I don't let myself believe I actually have a shot, that would just be so pathetic and self-loathing."

"I'm sorry, b. I really wasn't trying to make fun of you. I just—in my queer little heart, I have to believe that anything's possible when it comes to romance. Or else I'd literally shoot myself in the face."

"No I know. I'm sorry too."

July 2019

We park and unbuckle our seatbelts.

"Ready?"

"Hold on b, I can't find my wallet." Leggy rummages through the central console, tossing empty cans of Red Bull and blunt wrappers into the backseat.

Two teenage boys loitering in front of the store watch us through the windshield with smirks across their faces.

"Aha!" Leggy pulls out her wallet. "I'm ready, let's go."

"Wait. I'll go, you stay here."

"Why?"

"Cuz it looks like those boys are gonna say something to you, and like, I'd rather not."

"Them?" Leggy points at the boys and laughs. "They're like 12. I'd love to see them step up."

"Oh my god—shit, wait!"

She opens her door and steps out. "Come on, b."

"Shit. Fuck." I quickly untuck my shirt and hop out of the car.

I keep my eyes on the ground as we walk past the boys and into the store. Once we're inside, they burst into laughter.

Leggy squeezes my arm. "You good, b?"

"Yeah. Are you?"

"Yeah. I'm gonna go get my Red Bull."

"Okay, I'm gonna go get cigarettes."

I step up to the counter. "Hi. Can I get two packs of...uh...er... the Marlboro Lights? 100's? Sorry."

"ID?"

"Yeah, sorry." I take out my wallet and pull out my ID. "Oh and can I get her Red Bull, too?"

Leggy sets her Red Bull down on the counter. "You sure, b?"

"Yeah, I just—I wanna get out of here."

"24.67."

"Okay. Thank you. Sorry." I slide my card into the chip reader.

"Receipt?"

"No, I'm good."

"You're all set."

I stick a hand in my pocket as we walk out the door and I pinch my thigh as hard as I can. Leggy unlocks the car.

"Fuckin disgusting!"

Leggy turns around. "Excuse me?"

One of the boys steps forward. "Yeah, you're fucking disgusting! Stay home!"

Leggy laughs. "Love that confidence on you! It's actually really impressive considering you're 12 and you have a baby penis."

The boy lunges at her and his friend holds him back. "Get the fuck outta here *tranny cunt!*"

"With pleasure!"

We get back in the car and Leggy slams her door. "I'm sorry, but I had to. It was just too fucking easy." She pulls out of the parking spot sharply and we speed off. "How are you, though? Hey?"

"I, uh—" My voice cracks. "I'm fucking shook, to be honest with you."

"Are you mad at me? I had my pepper spray, we were fine."

"I'm not mad at anyone right now. I'm just like, really profoundly sad."

"Aw, b."

"No, oh my god, this isn't about me." I wipe at my eyes. "I just feel bad. Like, I love you a lot and it genuinely breaks my heart."

"You don't have to feel sorry for me."

"No I know. I know you can deal. It's just fucked up that you're so used to it."

"Yeah."

"I think I also just forgot what it was like. Living with you. Stepping out in public and fucking feeling it. It's beyond."

"It's not *that* bad." She smiles at me. "For me, at least. Like, I'm really out here just vibing."

"I know. How the fuck do you do it?"

"I just know in my heart with so much certainty that I'm the shit. And getting heckled at by little boys and old Asian ladies isn't gonna rattle my enormous fucking ego like that."

I laugh.

"Am I right or am I right?"

"You're right. You're so right." I roll down my window and light a cigarette.

"That stirred something up for you though, huh?"

"Yeah, I was like suddenly in 7th grade again with shoulder-length hair and a tangerine V-neck and it wasn't cute."

She smiles and reaches for my cigarette. "I wish we'd known each other back then. Do you ever think about that?"

"Oh my god, can you imagine?"

June 21, 2020

I stare into the bathroom mirror, drunk, zoning out to the familiarity of my own face. Until finally I achieve this disembodied meditative state where time and space cease to exist and there's absolutely nothing on my mind.

And then, an interruption. A thought that'd been bobbing around in the periphery of my consciousness gets thrust into the spotlight.

Call Leggy. Return her FaceTime. Stop being a douche.

—

"Hey bitch."

"Oh my goodness, he's back from the dead!"

"I know, I'm really sorry. I, uh—I wanted to apologize for being so hard to reach lately."

"It's fine! I'm just glad to see you. How are you?"

"No, it's not fine. I've been a really shitty friend and it's quarantine and you mean a lot to me."

"B, are you drunk?"

"I mean yeah, but don't let that take away from anything I've just said."

She laughs. "I miss you. When am I gonna see you?"

"Oh well actually Didier just went back to my dad's house—it's a long story. But yeah, we have a spare room right now if you wanna come over for a few days."

"Oh shit, forreal?"

"Yeah, so please come whenever. I really desperately need to hang out with someone other than my mom."

"Does she still have corona?"

"Yes and no. But like, at this point, who even gives a shit?"

"Honestly, I wanna get infected just to get it over with. Like please cough directly into my butthole."

"Bitch, when can you come?"

"Hmm, well right now I'm actually in Fresno."

"Ew, why?"

"I'm with some guy I met on Grindr. We've been like, having sex and ordering Postmates non-stop for five days. It's grotesque."

"That's hot."

"I can probably be in Palm Springs the day after tomorrow though? Is that okay?"

"Yes of course!"

"Oh my god okay, I'm so excited."

"Wait what about the guy?"

"Oh I'm so over it. I'd much rather see you."

"Where is he right now?"

"Sleeping right next to me." She switches to her front camera and pans over his half-naked body. "He takes Trazodone, out like a fucking light."

"Wait, stop, that's so awkward!"

"Do you wanna see his dick?"

"I mean, obviously, yeah, I want to see his dick."

June 22, 2020

I swiffer the kitchen floor while my mom loads groceries into the fridge.

"What are you gonna make for dinner tomorrow?"

"I don't know. What does Leggy like?"

"She's poor, she'll eat anything."

"Mm."

"She likes pseudo-healthy shit, like Caesar salads and plant-based meat. Avocados. Smoothies. Does that paint enough of a picture?"

"Not really, but, whatever."

"You'll figure it out."

My mom shuts the fridge door and turns to me. "Matheus."

"Yeah?"

"I want you to know that I plan on searching Leggy's bag when she gets here."

"Okay..."

"For Vyvanse."

"Yeah, I figured."

"That's my one condition. If she wants to stay in this house, I have to be absolutely sure that there's gonna be no—"

"I said it's fine, okay? I get it. I'm not tripping about Leggy bringing Vyvanse, she doesn't even take it anymore."

"Well just let her know, because if I find any, I will flush them."

"Okay."

June 23, 2020

My mom dumps the rest of the wine into her glass, and then she licks the last few dribbles off the neck of the bottle. I mouth an apology to Leggy across the table.

"So Matheus tells me you're in cosmetology school. That must be fun."

"Actually no, it's just as boring as regular school."

"Oh no, that's too bad!"

"No, it's all good. I'm actually really passionate about it, I just hate learning shit I already know."

"Do you have anything that could help me with my skin?"

Leggy leans in across the table and studies my mom's face. "What do you mean though?"

"Like, do you see all these lines? And the crepiness?"

"Ms. Nucci, your skin looks great! Like, seriously, there's nothing for me to fix."

"How is it possible that you're not seeing this?"

"I am seeing it, I just mean—it's age. And that's okay! Like it's better not to fight it too much, or else...you might end up really sad and confused about your appearance?"

I spit out my chicken. "You're an old hag and you need to *accept it!*"

"No that's not what I meant!"

"It's fine, I know I'm old."

"Ms. Nucci, I'm so sorry! Like I genuinely think you're hot and I really didn't mean to imply that you should give up on your appearance or anything like that! **Shit.**"

I laugh. "Oh my god, we love a messy first impression."

"I know, your mom totally hates me now. I'll be lucky to make it to dessert."

"I don't hate you! I think you're a lot of fun, actually. And I'm really glad you're here to see Matheus. He'll probably never admit this, but he missed you a lot."

"Aw, b! I love you guys. This house has a fabulous energy and I feel really welcome here, so, thank you. I'm very grateful for all this."

"I, uh—" I clear my throat. "I actually have a little announcement that I've been waiting to share with both of you, and I think now is as good a time as any."

"Okay."

"So, a few weeks ago, I started writing a book."

"Oh!"

"Yeah, it's like a quarantine memoir thing with some flashbacks to last summer. And both of you are in it, a lot. We're probably in it right now."

My mom scowls. "Why would you say that?"

"Because...it's good news? I'm writing a book."

Leggy frowns and scrapes at her plate.

"Why is nobody happy for me?"

"It's just weird. It's a weird thing to say, Matheus."

"Yeah b, I don't know if I'm totally comfortable with that."

"Oh come on! *I'm writing a book!*"

"Your writing, it's sort of...exhibitionist."

Leggy nods.

"I mean I'll show it to you guys before it gets published, obvi. And you can tell me if anything crosses the line."

"Yeah but that's the thing, it always has to cross the line with you. Like Baby Teeth—"

"Baby Teeth was a massive failure, this is gonna be nothing like Baby Teeth. It's like, lighter and funnier and I'm taking myself a lot less seriously."

"Okay. I mean, I can't stop you. Just don't make me look like an idiot again."

"Leggy? What about you, do you have anything to say?"

"Yeah, just don't make me look like an idiot."

June 24, 2020

Leggy twists around in the pool like a baby otter while I sit on the lawn and smoke a cigarette.

"I feel bad."

She dunks her head underwater and shoots back up. "What?"

"I said I feel bad."

"What's wrong?"

"I feel like I should be showing you around town. And like, getting us into wild gay shenanigans."

"Oh that's so not the vibe for this vacay. Like, I'm literally just using you for your pool." She swims over to me and reaches for my cigarette.

"Oh dude, you know what we can do? I have HBO here, so I can finally show you Euphoria. Would you be down?"

She takes a long drag from my cigarette and exhales with a coughing fit.

"Bitch why do you always do that? You're not supposed to hit it like a joint."

She pounds on her chest. "I don't know. My brain keeps telling me to."

"So...Euphoria? What do you think? It doesn't have to be now—"

"Maybe. I don't know, b."

"I thought you were dying to see it?"

"I mean yeah. But like, everyone says it's really heavy. And I'm trying to keep things light, you know?"

"No yeah, that's totally fine." I put out my cigarette. "I'm gucci with whatever you want to do."

"Get in the pool with me!"

"I will. I'm just—I live here, so I'm not as impressed with it as you are."

—

Leggy shuts my laptop and smiles up at me. "I like it."

"You don't have to like it, it's just a first draft. I just wanted you to see I wasn't talking shit."

"No, like, it's really good."

"Nothing like Baby Teeth, right?"

"Yeah the tone is completely different. Way less heavy. You can kinda just fall into it without too much effort."

"That's pretty much what I was going for."

"But are you sure you're gonna be okay sharing this with people? Like, it's *so* personal. And all the stuff about your mom..."

"I'm not worried about it. To be honest, the only person I'm nervous about showing it to is my dad. But it's fine, I think I'm just gonna tell him it's semi-fictional or something."

"Yeah, I think that's the move."

"Do you have any notes?"

"Um...I mean obviously there's no plot."

"Right."

"So, I think it runs the risk of being a little too **broad.** Does that make sense?"

"Totally, yeah."

"And I was there for all this shit, so I don't have a problem following it, but maybe other people would need a little more context? I don't know, I know that the choppy thing is kind of your style."

"Yeah."

"But I loved it, seriously. I thought it was really clean and refreshing and like actually funny."

"Okay now say something negative again."

She smirks. "Okay there was one thing."

"What?"

"Your biphobia is like, popping off the page."

I laugh. "Oh my god, I'm so glad you caught that!"

"Girl, how could I not?"

"Is it really that bad?"

"It's just like, unnecessary."

"Shit."

"Like what is it accomplishing? It's just spreading more hate."

"Mhmm."

"I just don't want you to get demolished on Twitter, that's all I'm saying."

"Yeah..." I sit up in bed and hug my knees. "Okay now tell me something nice again. Let's keep going back and forth."

June 25, 2020

Leggy scrapes some wax out of a little glass jar with a dental tool. "So when I say go, you're gonna put your mouth right here and start breathing in. But don't touch anything else, cuz it's gonna be super hot. Okay?"

"Okay." My mom pulls back her hair. "Let's do this shit."

Leggy fires up her butane torch and blasts the bulb of her dab rig, turning it around in the flame until the glass glows red. My mom covers her ears and squints.

"Ok, now!"

My mom brings her lips up to the mouthpiece as Leggy swirls the wax around the inside of the hot bulb. The water chamber rolls to a bubble as she inhales.

"Faster! Breathe in faster!"

My mom pulls away and hacks out a plume of smoke. She stands and doubles over and retches uncontrollably. Leggy finishes the dab.

"Mom are you okay?"

"Vitamin Water!"

I hand her my Vitamin Water and she downs it between stifled coughs.

"How do you feel?"

"Shiii. I feel like…I'm already way too high."

"That sounds about right."

"Matheus, why have you never shown me this before? This wax bong contraption is magical."

"It's called dabbing, and it's fucking atrocious. It's literally like cooking drugs."

Leggy scoffs. "You're also *cooking drugs* when you smoke a joint. It's called *combustion."*

"True. I don't know, dabbing just hits me way too heavy."

"B, it's literally the cleanest form of weed you can get. Pure THC concentrate."

"No I know, I'm not trying to argue with you. I'm just saying for me, personally."

"Well I was about to ask if you wanted a dab, but I guess not?"

"No yeah, I'm good."

—

"Mm, Ms. Nucci, is there bacon in this?"

My mom looks up from her plate. "There's some chunks of ham in the beans. Do you not eat ham?"

"Yeah, sorry, I'm a little grossed out by pork. But it's okay, I can just pick them out."

"Hm."

We look down at our plates and continue eating in silence. Outside, the nightly firework show begins.

Bang!

Bang!

My mom clears her throat. "Leggy I hope the fireworks haven't been keeping you up too much."

"Oh I barely notice them anymore. It's a million times worse in Santa Ana."

"Really?" I turn to her. "Is it like, every night?"

"Every night, all night, right outside my window."

"Oh damn. Here it's not that bad, but it's definitely getting worse. Right, Mom?"

She nods.

"It's funny—when it first started, we thought it was actually the neighbor passive-aggressively slamming their back door cuz we were smoking too much."

My mom laughs. "It's true! It really sounded like that."

"That's funny."

"And you've heard the conspiracy theory, right?"

Leggy furrows her brows. "What conspiracy theory?"

My mom and I turn to each other and beam.

"What conspiracy theory!"

"About the fireworks. It's been all over Twitter for days."

"I literally left all social media this summer except for Instagram so I have no idea what you're talking about."

"Okay so basically they're saying Trump is behind it."

"Trump is setting off the fireworks?"

"No!" I laugh. "Obviously he's not doing it himself. But there's these crates full of cheap fireworks mysteriously showing up on street corners across the country, mostly in black neighborhoods. Nobody knows who's doing it. There's videos of this happening and everything."

"So?"

Bang!

"So, the idea is, you've got these black neighborhoods

popping off with fireworks every night, keeping everyone awake. It's classic psychological warfare. And the ultimate goal is to make BLM look dangerous and unhinged."

"Mm."

Bang!

Bang!

"And—and it also serves as a way to relegitimize the police, cuz you've got people calling the cops on the fireworks, and then, surprise, they can go and arrest some black guy for it."

"Yeah but b, the fireworks started way before George Floyd."

"Yeah, but, still. There's an election coming up, and the plan's always been to fuck with black voters."

Leggy squints at me.

"You don't look convinced."

"I'm not."

"Well, when me and my mom first heard it, it made a lot of sense to us."

"I don't know, it just seems like a lot of hoops to jump through."

"Yeah."

"I mean obviously past Republican presidents have pulled some crazy shit to disenfranchise black people, but like, *a crate of fireworks on every corner?* I don't see it b, I'm sorry. I don't think Trump could even pull that off, actually."

Bang!

Bang!

Bang!

"So what do you think it is? Have you never wondered?"

Leggy shrugs. "Honestly? I think people are just blowing

off steam."

"Mhmm."

"That just seems like the most logical explanation to me."

—

"Close the door, Matheus." My mom sits up in bed.

I step into her room and close the door behind me. "What is it?"

"She's been here for **three days.** I need my house back."

"No I know. I'm like, a husk of a person right now."

"So can you please make sure she goes home tomorrow?"

"Okay but I can't just outright ask her to leave."

"Why not?"

"Because that would be weird and rude. It needs to happen organically."

"What about me? Is this not rude to me?"

I sigh. "Okay, I'll handle it."

"It's too much, Matheus. Too much social interaction."

"Yeah, I said I'll fucking handle it."

June 26, 2020

"Okay wait b, pause it."

I pick up the remote and pause the episode of Euphoria. "What is it?"

"I just need to stop and debrief for a second, is that okay?"

"Sure."

"Okay so, Jules. It's kind of a lot."

"Right."

"I feel like she's literally the first realistic trans girl character I've ever seen on TV, and I should be really happy about that, but I'm not. I'm like, cringing."

"Mhmm."

"I don't know. I wanted real, but this might be *too* real."

"So do you want to stop watching?"

"No, let's keep going. I just wanted to take a second and talk it through, cuz I'm actually feeling kind of guilty about it."

"Guilty about what?"

"Because I should be enjoying this show and I'm not."

"Then let's stop."

"No! Please, let's just finish the episode."

"Um...okay." I chuckle. "Whatever you want." I pick up the remote and hit play.

My mom walks in and starts fumbling with the weed jars on the counter. "Matheus?"

"What?"

"Can you roll me a joint? It looks like I'm out of pre-rolls..."

I groan. "After this episode? Please?"

"Why can't you roll me a joint and watch at the same time?"

"Cuz I'm tired and I don't fucking feel like it."

"Excuse me?" She steps in front of the TV.

"Mom, move."

"You think you can walk all over me just because your friend is here?"

"Please, can we not do this in front of Leggy?—"

"I'm asking you to roll me a fucking joint here!"

"Mom shut the fuck up you're embarrassing yourself."

"Hey b, it's okay. We can stop watching this, I'm not that into it."

"Oh my **GOD!**" I throw my hands in the air. "Yeah, I'm done. That was it, that was my limit. So, fuck all of you. I'm out."

"Matheus if you walk away without rolling this joint, you're never touching my weed ever again."

"Great! That'd be your first responsible parenting decision in 10 years!"

—

There's a knock on my bedroom door. "Hey b, can I come in?"

"Sure."

Leggy steps into my room and closes the door behind her. "Hi."

"Hi."

"So that was a moment."

"Yeah."

"Are you okay?"

"I'm really overwhelmed. But I shouldn't have spoken to you like that, I'm sorry."

"No, you were right. I have been...difficult."

I look down at my hands.

"So. I think I'm gonna go home."

"If that's what you want."

"It's just starting to feel like I've overstayed my welcome."

"Yeah."

She purses her lips and glances around the room. "Okay. Bye, then."

"Wait, I'll walk you out and we can do this the right way."

"You don't have to do that."

"Yes, I do. Or else I'll literally start crying the second you leave."

"Yeah, I was already planning on crying in the car, so."

"Oh my god, can I just—" I stand up and give her a hug. *"I'm so fucking sorry."*

"Me too, b."

"Do you hate me?"

"Literally never."

"Shit." I wipe at my eyes. "What a gross feeling."

"I think there was just a lot of pressure on this visit."

"Yeah."

"It's a weird time."

"Really weird."

"But we're good, okay? The love is unconditional."

"I feel the exact same way."

"Good. Then we're solid."

I sigh. "Do you have all your shit packed?"

"Yeah. Lemme just say bye to your mom first."

"Oop, bad idea."

"Are you sure? I'd feel weird leaving without saying bye."

"No yeah, let's just go."

—

I take a seat at the little white table by the pool and I light a cigarette. "She just left, by the way. It's over."

My mom ignores me and continues scrolling on her phone.

"So you're just gonna ignore me now?"

Silence.

"I'm sorry. What I said was really unfair. Cuz you've given me this awesome life where I can just do whatever I want and not have to worry about money, and all you ask in return is for me to roll you a joint every once in a while. So. I should just shut up and roll you the fucking joint, cuz it's literally the least I could do."

I study her face as she sets down her phone and stares out over the pool. And then she reaches into her robe pocket, lights a keef-crusted blunt, and passes it to me unceremoniously.

"Oh shit." I smile and take the blunt. "I guess you were bluffing about cutting me off?"

"All I want is peace, Matheus."

"Oh my god, me too."

"You're never inviting anyone over ever again. This house is now a visitor-free zone."

"I'm so down. Cheers to that." I hold up my cigarette.

"Cheers."

September 2019

You can dance, you can jive, having the time of your life

Meatlorfer grabs my hand and tries to pull me up off the couch. *"Come dance with me!"*

"I'm not drunk enough to dance in front of straight people!"

"Come on, we never have any fun together!"

"Then go away and let me chug!"

"God, you're so fucking depressing!" She lets go of me and boogies back to the throng of dancers.

I turn to Leggy. "Let's go get another drink!"

—

I push aside a curtain of yellow streamers as we enter the kitchen. I go straight for the bottle of vodka in the freezer while Leggy fixes her hair in the reflection of the microwave.

"Who the fuck invited all these cishets to my going-away party?"

"I think Meatlorfer just invited everyone from set."

"I hate everyone from set. I hate dancing. I hate 70's-themed parties." I take a long chug from the bottle. "Whatever happened to getting drunk on a park bench with a couple of besties and a homeless prostitute? Cuz like, that's where I shine conversationally and everyone knows it."

"No yeah, Meatlorfer's literally throwing a party for herself right now and pretending like it's for you."

I shriek. "Exactly!"

—

Meatlorfer sits down next to me on the porch steps. I reach out and light her cigarette.

"Thanks."

"Mhmm."

"I feel like you've been avoiding me all night. Is that just my impression?"

"It's just your impression."

"Good." She scoots over and wraps herself around my arm.

I chuckle. "What are you doing?"

"I'm gonna miss you. I'm gonna miss my little cigarette buddy."

"I'm gonna miss you too..."

"No you're not." She lets go of my arm. "You hate me."

"I don't **hate** you."

She smirks. "But I did something to piss you off, right? Apparently something really serious?"

"Meatlorfer—"

"Shut up, we need to talk about this right now before you leave thinking I'm some kind of monster."

"Dude, you already know what my issues are with you."

"Well apparently I don't, so, please enlighten me."

"I'm just—I'm massively disappointed by how little you gave a shit about Baby Teeth."

"That's bullshit!"

"Dude you can't sit there and tell me you worked your ass off for it, cuz you didn't. Like, you never even tried to understand my vision—"

"That's because you didn't **have** a vision! I'm sorry, but you didn't! You can't even tell me what your movie is **about!** As if there's some fucking super secret hidden meaning! It's all bullshit, dude."

I scoff.

"I know you think your script was this masterpiece and that Meatlorfer the big bad director came in and shat all over it, but that's not what happened, okay? I made your movie the way you wrote it, and if you're not happy with the way it turned out, then maybe it's because your script wasn't that incredible to begin with. Sorry."

"Is that really what you think?" I bite my lip.

"I think you take yourself too seriously as an artist."

"Yeah, I'm uh..." I stand and stomp out my cigarette. "I'm gonna go, cuz you're an abusive piece of shit, and I don't really want to be your friend anymore."

"Okay, bye."

"Yep." I open the front door.

—

"Order 351 and 352!"

"I'll get it, b."

"Okay, thanks."

Leggy grabs our trays at the counter and brings them back

to our booth. I watch as she unwraps the foil from her burrito and takes a big wet bite.

"Stop, why are you staring at me?" She covers her mouth.

I smile. "Your hair. You look like you're from the 70's, and it's kinda making it look like the whole restaurant is in the 70's."

"Oh, trippy." She turns around and scans the empty dining area. A couple of freshmen order chicken tacos at the register.

"Leggy."

"Yeah?"

"Tell me what we're gonna do when we get home."

"Mm. I was just thinking of taking a fat dab, watching some Schitt's Creek, and then passing out on the couch. The usual."

"Oof." I close my eyes.

"We can do something else if you want?"

"No, that's beautiful. The usual sounds amazing."

July 2020

July 2, 2020

My mom opens the blinds. "It's 3pm Matheus, up up up."

I turn over in bed and blink up at her. "What?"

"We're doing a Costco run today. Did you forget?"

"Just go without me."

"No, you have to come! Or else you complain about how I don't buy good shit."

"I'm serious, Mom, I'm not feeling well right now. I think I might have corona."

"That's impossible, we have antibodies."

"That's...not how it works."

"Hm. What are your symptoms?"

"I don't know. I'm like, braindead. Headache. And I had diarrhea last night."

"Shit." She touches my forehead. "No fever, though. Any respiratory symptoms?"

"No."

"Nausea? Aches? Loss of smell?"

"No."

"You probably don't have corona."

"I just don't feel like going out, is that okay?"

"Okay. But I don't want to hear any whining about groceries

when I get back."

"Mom—"

July 3, 2020

"I think I'm depressed again."

"What?" My mom looks up from her phone.

"I said I think I'm depressed."

"What happened?"

"Nothing **happened.** You know that's not how it works."

"Mm."

"But I think Leggy's visit kinda sealed the deal. It's like, an energy hangover."

"Mm." She nods and looks back down at her phone.

"Have you really not noticed that I've been acting different?"

"Uh...I don't know. I thought you were sick?"

"Yeah, at first I thought it was corona. And then I thought maybe it was the tonsil cancer finally metastasizing to my brain, but I didn't want to annoy you with any of that."

She sighs.

"Exactly."

"It sounds like you're just trying to pick a fight with me right now and I don't understand why."

"I'm depressed. You can't take me seriously."

"Well I get depressed sometimes too, but I don't go around trying to take other people down with me like an odious little shit."

I scoff.

"Look, I already asked you if you wanted to see Dr. Chinn weeks ago and you said no, so, there's really nothing else I can do to help you."

"Yeah, forget it. I don't know why I talk to you about anything."

July 4, 2020

The fireworks reach a terrifying crescendo just after dark. We step outside to witness it, cupping our ears, squinting up at the chaos in the sky.

"This is too much for me!"

"What!"

"This is too much! I'm back going inside!"

July 6, 2020

My mom opens the oven and slides in a tray of frozen spanako-pita. That one copper IUD commercial comes on TV and I break out into a little side-step dance.

"Look at you. Happy happy."

"I'm not happy, I'm just really high."

July 7, 2020

"Hi, Dr. Chinn, can you hear me?"

"Yes, hi."

"Hi."

"It's nice to see you again, Matheus."

"Yeah, you too. I have to admit, this is a little weird for me. Doing this over video chat."

"Have you chosen a good spot?"

"Yeah, I'm just in my garage. I didn't want my mom to over-hear us."

"Is that something you're concerned about?"

"I mean yeah, cuz I plan on talking shit."

Dr. Chinn laughs. "Have you been in quarantine with your mother this entire time?"

"Yeah."

"Uh-oh."

"Right? You get it. You get why I'm here."

"You tell me. What brings you back to therapy?"

I sigh. "How long has it been since we've seen each other?"

"Like two years, a little over two years."

"Am I supposed to fill you in on everything that's happened to me in the last two years?"

"Only if you want to."

"I don't want to."

"That's fine."

"So, basically, I'm depressed again. And it's extremely annoy-ing, because I've been trying to write this thing and I really need to not be depressed for it. And it's just super demoralizing because I have no idea how long this episode is gonna last."

"Mm."

"It could be two weeks, it could be two months, it could be fucking *six* months. And I can't do that again, you know? That's like, a sizeable chunk of my life wasted."

"Are you looking to get back on antidepressants?"

"I don't know. If it comes to that, yeah. But hopefully not."

"Mhmm. And how's your health anxiety?"

"Terrible, thanks for asking. And it's gotten a lot worse in quarantine, cuz I'm just sitting on my ass all day catastrophizing."

"And is it still—? What was it? Brain cancer?"

"Tonsil cancer. I'm back to esophagus-heart-lungs."

"Ah. No breathing exercises for you, then."

I chuckle. "Yeah, exactly."

"So tell me more about your tonsil troubles."

"Well this time it's a little different, cuz there's an actual physical tumor growing out of my right tonsil. And it's been there for like a year and a half, and I can feel it scraping against the back of my tongue pretty much constantly. So. Death is imminent. And every waking second of my life is weighed down with overwhelming dread."

"That sounds exhausting."

"It is."

"Have you seen a doctor?"

"I went to two doctors and they both said there was nothing wrong. Can you believe the audacity?"

"So why didn't you go to a third doctor?"

"Uh..." I smirk.

"Why stop at two if you know something's wrong?"

"Dr. Chinn, I know you think I'm full of shit, but—"

"I don't think you're full of shit. I think you have an anxiety disorder, and anxiety makes people think in unproductive ways."

"Yeah."

"And your mother—I'm assuming she's still completely useless when it comes to talking through this stuff."

"Oh yeah. Honestly, if I started going off about my tumor, she'd probably tell me to shut the fuck up and go fuck myself."

"Right. So, given all that, it's really no surprise you've ended up depressed. Especially in these times. It's a pretty natural response to this kind of sustained anxiety."

"I don't care if it's a natural response, I just need my brain back. Like at a certain point the anhedonia is just unacceptable. I'm half alive."

"I hear you. And I'll tell you what, before we get started on the Lexapro, I think it might be a good idea for us to do a little refresh on your CBT exercises and see if anything sticks. How does that sound?"

"Oh my god, yes, give me all the fucking CBT. I've forgotten everything, I'm terrible."

August 2019

Meatlorfer pounds on the bathroom door. "GINAAAAA! GINA QUIT FUCKING PLAYING!"

"Dude what the fuck is going on?"

"We're fucked. Gina's locked herself in the bathroom and she won't tell me where anything is and we have 10 minutes until the next shot."

"Okay. This screaming and pounding method clearly isn't helping, so, I'm gonna need you to step away and I'll take care of this."

"You?" Meatlorfer scoffs. "The one who's always in a crisis is now the crisis manager?"

"Yeah, it's funny how life comes full circle like that."

"You have 5 minutes before I break down this door. Less than 5 minutes."

"Fine." I knock on the door. "Gina, this is Matheus. Can I come in?"

"Is Meatlorfer with you?"

"No, she finally fucked off."

I hear the click of the door unlocking, and I step in slowly.

I find Gina sitting with her back up against the wall hugging her knees and staring into oblivion.

I close the door behind me. "What do we have here? A little mental health crisis? It's about damn time." I take a seat on the floor.

"I...fucked something up."

"You can tell me and I promise I won't freak out, whatever it is."

Gina buries her face in her hands. "I fucked up the lemon meringue pie. It got banged up in my car."

"In a way that would be like, unacceptable for the camera?"

Her face twists in agony.

"Well first of all, I just want to say that I'm not mad, and I'm really happy that you're working on this project with us. I'd literally rather have no one else on the team."

She starts sobbing.

"I think, whatever happened, we all know it's not due to negligence. Cuz literally no one cares more about this film than you. And I will actually throw hands if anyone tries to blame you for this."

"I'm so fucked."

"Dude, I promise there's a solution."

"No. We can't switch around the scenes because Cynthia needs to be at an audition in Van Nuys at 3:30. It's fucked. It's all fucked."

"What if we tried to fix the pie?"

"You can't. It's literally so ugly."

"Is it still in one piece though?"

"I mean, yeah?"

"Well then fuck it, we need to try. Come on."

"Okay. *Shit.* I'm coming." She wipes at her eyes.

"Where is it?"

"In the fridge, bottom drawer."

I swing into the kitchen and grab the pie out of the fridge. "Itziana?"

"Yeah?"

"I'm gonna need you to help us with some emergency surgery on this pie."

"Oh shit, okay."

I set the pie down on the counter and pop off the plastic lid, which takes most of the meringue with it. *"Fuck."*

Gina covers her mouth in horror. *"Oh god!"*

"Okay, let's think. Itziana, do you have anything that kind of looks like meringue?"

"I can check the pantry, but, I'm pretty sure I didn't bring anything."

"Okay, Gina, I need you to go check the bathrooms for shaving cream. And if they don't have any, go to the garage and look for spackle or something."

"Copy." She sprints off.

I grab a knife and start finagling the pie out of its tin.

"Oh!—" Itziana reaches into the pantry. "Marshmallow fluff!"

"Holy shit, that's perfect. How are your frosting skills?"

"Not the best, but, I've done it before."

"Do you think it's possible to make this look presentable?"

"I'm gonna try." She grabs a spatula. "This is like, the most exciting thing that's happened to me all week."

"I'm glad one of us is having fun."

Meatlorfer storms into the kitchen. "Where the fuck is Gina? IS THAT MY PIE? STOP! I NEED THIS IN 5 MINUTES!" She pulls on Itziana's arm.

Itziana drops her spatula and looks back at Meatlorfer in disgust. "Bitch, what the actual fuck?"

"Dude, she's just trying to fix it. It got bumped around in Gina's car."

Itziana raises her spatula. "I'm sorry but if I'm gonna do this, this bitch needs to leave the kitchen."

"Fine. But after you do this, you're out. And I'm making sure you never step foot on another Chapman set ever again."

"That's not even a thing! Yeah, walk away bitch, that's exactly what I thought." She shakes her head. "Oh my god, dude, your friend is fucking grotesque."

"Yeah, she's literally the worst."

"God-fucking-damnit."

"Are you okay? You don't have to keep doing this if you don't want to."

"No yeah, I'm fine. Let's do this shit."

—

I watch as Gina hands off the pie to Cynthia.

"Oh my god, my famous lemon meringue! Thank you, darling."

"You got it?"

"Yeah, I think so." Cynthia brings the pie up to her face and sniffs it. "What is this? Did you guys make it?"

"It's marshmallow fluff."

"The whole thing is marshmallow fluff?"

"No." Gina chuckles. "There's a pie under there somewhere. Don't worry about it, it's a camera thing."

"Ah." Cynthia nods. "That makes sense. Well, it looks delicious. Very Martha Stewart in that homemade sort of way."

Gina beams. "Yeah? Thank you!"

"Do you think I could try a little piece after this shot?"

July 8, 2020

"You know who I wish was my mom?"

"Who?"

"Dr. Chinn."

"That's nice. You should go for it."

"Did you hear us yesterday? In the garage?"

"No, why?"

"I thought maybe you'd try to eavesdrop."

"I have no interest in spying on your therapy sessions, Matheus, I already listen to your bitching all day."

"You really don't, though. There's actually a lot I don't talk to you about."

"Really?"

"Yeah, really."

"So when are you getting back on antidepressants?"

"That's kind of a hostile thing to ask someone."

"It's not hostile, it's a genuine question I have."

"I don't know. She asked if I wanted to get back on Lexapro and I was like, lol ideally no cuz I need to be sharp for this book I'm writing. So she was like, okay, let's just get back into the CBT exercises and see if that helps."

"Mm. Which one is CBT again?"

"Cognitive behavioral therapy. Remember, the one I did in rehab? With all the little tricks and spells?"

"Oh, yeah. The one that isn't bullshit."

"Yeah, exactly, the one that isn't bullshit."

"Well I think you sound better already. More upbeat."

"No literally, watch me soar out of this depression pit."

July 9, 2020

The dogs stop to sniff a shrub.

My mom pulls down her mask. "I think I'm gonna ask Manuel to plant a lemon tree in the yard. Everyone has a lemon tree except for us."

"Mom, your mask."

"There's no one here!"

"Still. People could be watching."

"Goddamn..." She slips her mask back on. "It must be really not fun to be you."

"Oh it's terrible. Constant agony."

July 10, 2020

"Look what I bought!" My mom prances into the living room holding up a white paper bag.

"Oh fuck, the blunts?"

"Yeah!"

"Bitch, every time you come home with blunts it means you did something wrong."

She laughs. "No! These are celebratory blunts, not apology blunts."

"What are we celebrating?"

She sits down next to me on the couch. "Okay, so, do you remember that man I've been talking to?"

"What man?"

"You know, the one I've been texting all summer? The guy I went to high school with?"

"Oh wow, it's still the same guy? That's so random."

"Yeah. So...he invited me to his friend's ranch in Tennessee. And I think I'm gonna go."

"When?"

"In four days."

"No way."

"I know right?"

"No, Mom, you can't go. This is a complete mental health disaster for me."

"Don't do that."

"I'm sorry, but now is not the time to be leaving me alone with my diseased mind."

"Matheus—"

"And I don't even know who he is! How am I supposed to send you off across the country when I don't know anything about this man?"

She laughs. "You're not my father. You're not **sending me off** anywhere."

"I mean, whatever. Obviously I have no say in this, so."

"I think it'll be fun, for both of us. Think of it as a little vacation."

"Mm."

"I'll leave you plenty of money and weed and food. You won't even need me for anything."

"Fine. But don't be surprised if you come home to find the dogs feasting on my rotting corpse."

"Matheus!"

"I'm sorry, but it's true. I could die. **You** could die. It's basically inevitable that one of us will die."

July 11, 2020

I actually took a cognitive test very recently, when I, uh, when I was—you know the radical left was saying, is he all there, is he all there? And I proved I was all there because I aced it, I aced the test…

My mom looks over at me and cackles. I smile back weakly.

And Biden should take the same exact test. A very standard test, I took it at Walter Reed Medical Center in front of doctors, and they were all very surprised. They said, that's an incredible thing…

"It's a fucking dementia test! He's going around bragging about passing a dementia test!"

"Mom, can I change the channel?"

"What! No way! This is top-tier comedy."

"I'm so tired of this Trump shit."

"Well, I'm not, so."

"Yeah, that's because you're a **white neoliberal.**"

She laughs. "A **what?**"

"You heard me, a **white neoliberal.**"

"Explain to me what that is."

"It's what Obama was, but **white.**"

"I think Obama did great."

"Obama conducted airstrikes on Libya to feel relevant."

"Maybe Libya deserved it?"

"I'm gonna go watch TV in my room."

"Wait, come back! Explain white neoliberal!"

July 12, 2020

We sit up in bed and flip through my mom's old photo album.

"What year was this?"

"It was my 15th birthday, so...'86."

"I mean most of the fashion is just haggard. Like, what is this, a pilgrim frock? Multiple people are straight-up wearing pilgrim frocks."

"Lots of young girls would wear that kind of dress to parties. It was considered classy and chaste."

"But not you."

"No of course not, I was cool as fuck."

"Okay but why are you wearing a white wedding dress on your 15th birthday?"

"It's not a wedding dress! It's just white, with lots of tulle."

"And the bows?"

"The bows were a must. The bigger the bow, the badder the bitch. Bow here, bow there, bow anywhere."

"Oh my god. Just turn the page, please."

"Oh wait, that's him!" She points at a young man in a ruffled shirt caught unaware on the outskirts of a group shot.

"That?"

"Yeah."

"Well he clearly wasn't hot enough to be in your friend group. What a little nerd bitch!"

"Yeah, honestly, I barely knew him back then. He was only there cuz I invited the whole class."

"Who would've guessed, 35 years later, you'd be traveling all the way to Tennessee in the midst of a pandemic to bang this little man?"

"Not in his wildest dreams, he says."

"That's so pathetic. All men are so pathetic."

"Mm."

"I don't understand how you're attracted to him."

"I don't know, Matheus. Tastes change. It's not always about...*hotness.*"

"That sounds like bullshit but okay."

"What's bullshit? You think I'm faking my attraction to him?"

"Actually, yeah. I think you're tryna be like, *look at me, I'm blind to ugliness and it makes me so evolved.* Fuck outta here."

"Matheus if all the hot people got together with hot people and all the ugly people got together with ugly people, there would be no fun in anything."

"Ha! So you admit he's ugly!"

She clicks her tongue.

"You just got so exposed, how embarrassing for you."

July 13, 2020

My mom sifts through her closet. "Should I pack a rain jacket?"

"In the middle of summer?"

"It's in the mountains, though. The **Smoky** Mountains."

"Is that supposed to mean anything to me?"

"Whatever, you're not being very helpful." She pulls a black Northface jacket off the hook and tosses it over her bed.

"You know what you should bring?"

"What?"

"A sun hat. Something kinda rustic and ranchy."

"Oh fuck yeah. Rustic sun hat." She digs deeper into her closet.

"Hey, Mom?"

"What?"

"I was thinking, we should do something fun today."

"What do you mean?"

"I mean, when you inevitably get murdered in Tennessee, this is gonna be our last day together ever and I think we should do something fun and memorable."

"I'm not engaging with this right now." She puts on a straw sun hat and checks herself out in the mirror.

"I mean there's always a chance. How would you want to spend today if you knew it was our last?"

"I don't know. The shit we do every day? Smoke and eat garbage and watch garbage TV."

"How about a poignant new memory that'll haunt me forever after your death?"

"Please stop talking about my death. You're putting it out into the universe."

"I don't think that's how it works, but okay."

July 14, 2020

"Oh, right here. This is United."

I pull up to the curb and we park behind a young couple hugging goodbye.

"Do you have all your shit? Mask? Phone?"

"Yeah, I think so."

"Is it okay if I don't get out of the car? I look atrocious."

"Yeah that's fine." My mom unbuckles her seatbelt. "Take good care of the dogs, okay?"

"Have fun. Cut it up."

"I will." She leans over and hugs me.

"Oh my god, Mom, don't look now, but those two people in front of us are breaking down violently in tears."

"What?" She turns around. "Oh fuck, they saw me!"

"I told you not to look."

"I know, I shouldn't have!"

"I don't understand how anyone could cry in public like that. Honestly, it's kind of rude."

"Matheus what do I do? I have to get out of this car eventually."

"Stop, act natural."

"Okay."

"Let's just pretend we're having a conversation. Like,

conversation conversation."

"Conversation conversation."

"Conversation."

"Oh, conversation?"

"Yeah, exactly, conversation."

October 2019

Grand Canyon, Arizona

"Get closer to the edge. Like, step down on that rock."

"Just take the fucking picture, Matheus. It's giving me vertigo."

"Mkay, but you're gonna have to smile. Or at least wipe that constipated look off your face."

"Yeah, no, I can't do this. I need to get away from the precipice."

"Mom stop! Go back there, you're being so extra."

"There's no railing, Matheus! If I slip, I *die!*"

"Okay but what an iconic way to go, though. ***She fucking fell off the Grand Canyon.***"

"Gimme my phone. I'm done."

—

We sit outside a gift shop and watch the mass of tourists shuffle along the rim of the canyon. A Russian family in athletic wear argues loudly as they stop for a picture.

"Okay Mom, I'm just gonna say it—the Grand Canyon is kind of trash."

"Oh 100%."

"Like I'm sorry, but this is some third world-ass

infrastructure."

"No railing."

"No railing! I mean, come on."

"I just feel bad for all these people who came from other countries. There's no way you can make an entire vacation out of this."

"Right! I mean as a stop on a road trip like we're doing, I get it. But what would you even do in this town for more than two hours? Kill yourself? Throw yourself off the cliff?"

She laughs.

"But whatever, I'm glad we came."

"Me too."

"It's like one of those things you **have** to do, you know?"

"Yeah."

July 16, 2020

"So now you're home alone?"

"All alone. Two weeks—that'll actually be a new record for me. I've never been by myself that long."

"And how do you feel about that?"

"Honestly, Dr. Chinn, I'm shitting myself."

"Why? It sounds like the kind of thing you'd enjoy."

"It does, doesn't it? But no. Not like this."

"What are you scared might happen?"

"I'm not scared of something happening, I'm scared of **nothing** happening. I'm scared I'll get really profoundly bored and just end up fixating on my tonsil the entire time."

"Right."

"And what's gonna happen if I start death spiraling and there's no one here to pull me back into reality? I don't know. I can see this going really badly."

"Well, there's a big difference between **death spiraling** and actually facing these thoughts in a calm, analytical way."

"Right."

"The goal of therapy isn't to **block** the bad thoughts with constant distractions. It's about analyzing them, and seeing them for what they are, and guiding them down more constructive pathways. Does that make sense?"

"Yeah, it does. And that's exactly what I want, I want to learn how to face it without spiraling. Cuz ultimately my goal is to go see a specialist and stop smoking and actually address some of these very real and very alarming symptoms I'm having. I want that. I want to take something constructive out of all this."

"Exactly. Which is why I think these next two weeks are actually a great opportunity for you in your recovery. It's a time for some rest but it's also a time for some meaningful reflection, away from all the distractions associated with your mom."

"Yeah, you're right." I chuckle. "Damn."

"What?"

"No, it's just—I'm realizing how little work I've put into my recovery over the years."

She nods.

"I talk a big game, but, I really don't know shit about mental health. I'm not doing enough reflection. I'm not...trying hard enough. *Fuck.*"

"Well you're here now, so. And these kinds of realizations are part of the process."

"Yeah."

"How about this—I'm gonna give you a little homework assignment for this week. It's a writing exercise."

"Okay, fun."

"So when you get stuck on an intrusive thought, I want you to stop whatever you're doing and really listen to it, ask it questions, flesh it out. And then you're gonna write that thought down on a notecard and put it in a shoe box labeled *distortions.*"

I smirk. "Okay."

"Are you up for it?"

"It sounds wildly irresponsible, but, yeah. I'm putting my faith in the CBT gods."

July 17, 2020

I watch my naked body as I float in the pool, from a bird's eye view. Body hair plastered to my glistening wet skin. Penis bobbing gently on the surface of the water, gummy and insignificant like fish bait.

A plane descends into town directly overhead, and I wonder if they can see me the way I see myself now. I hope they can. I hope someone up there's enjoying it. Preferably someone important and heterosexual, like a pilot or a white middle-aged businessman. Or maybe someone I went to elementary school with, who knew me only as this stiff, arrogant, perfect little sissy boy.

I start jacking off.

November 2019

Kai stands stark naked at the foot of the bed and plays the bassoon. His big erection swings around as he dips and sways with the music.

When he finishes his piece, I clap a little sort of sarcastically.

"So yeah, that's what I'm working on right now."

"I like it!"

"Thanks." He chuckles. "It's not quite *perfect* yet, but..."

"Do you always get an erection when you play the bassoon? I imagine that gets kind of inconvenient on stage."

"It's you, dumbass! You're just so freakin cute." He crawls into bed and kisses me.

"Gross."

He pulls away. "What?"

I laugh. "No, not you! You're fine. I just mean like, ew, affection. Affection is gross."

"Do you not want me to kiss you? I know on Tinder you said you were asexual—"

"No yeah it's fine. Please do whatever you want with me."

"Are you sure? I don't want to push you."

"I know my boundaries. I'm basically okay with anything as long as you're not like, penetrating my butthole. And even that's negotiable."

"Okay."

"And I promise I'm not like a weird virgin or anything like that. I've **had** sex. A lot of sex, actually. I just really hate everything about it and I'll only do it if I absolutely have to."

"Right."

"That sounded weird. I'm never in a position where I **absolutely have to** have sex. It's just like, sometimes, if you want something from a man, you have to take a dick up the ass. Not that I want anything from you! Even though, yes, you are a weed dealer, and I'm definitely expecting to see some perks."

He laughs. "Yikes!"

"I'm sorry, can we start over? Hi, I'm Matheus and I'm a normal human boy."

"Hi. You're clearly way too cute for me. Are you sure you didn't swipe right on accident?"

"Oh my god, Kai, you're hot."

"Are you sure it's not just because I'm a drug dealer?"

"No! You're like a genuine snack."

"Have you noticed how I'm like, fat?"

"What if I told you I was into fat hairy Jewish guys?"

"Then I'd marry you."

"I don't wanna marry anyone. I think one day I might marry myself, like a self-wedding."

"That's kinda gay."

"You can kiss me again, by the way, I'm ready for this conversation to be over."

November 2019

Lakeway, Texas

House Hunting

Trixie Pope swings open the French doors and leads us out onto a palatial balcony. "Nice view of Lake Travis. Y'all could always trim these big oaks, but I personally love all that Spanish moss. *So antebellum.*"

My mom turns to me and beams. "What a view!"

"Yeah, it's nice. It's kind of a lot, though, isn't it?"

"What's a lot?"

"I don't know, it's just hard to believe we can afford all this. I'm like, what's the catch? Who died here?"

Trixie Pope shrieks. "Well aren't you just a little devil on your mama's shoulder! Shoo little devil, shoo!"

"I know, just ignore him. He doesn't like to see me happy."

—

"Me and my girlfriends, we're all extremely active in the Democratic Party around here. It's so important to get involved."

My mom nods. "Yes, absolutely."

"A lot of people don't know this, but Texas is shaping up to be a real swing state in the next few elections."

"Oh wow, wouldn't *that* be something?"

"It could happen. It really could. I mean, at least here in the Austin area, you never run into any Trump crazies or anything like that. Much less a *racist.*"

"Mm."

"Of course there's still the older generation. Like my mama, she's passed away, bless her heart. She had this *African-American* nurse in hospice, Berta, lovely woman. One day Berta comes up to me in the lobby, and she's like, *Miss Trixie, yo mudda's kicked me outta huh room and she be whoopin' and hollerin' obscenities at me!* And I was like, yep, that's Mama!"

My mom laughs weakly. "Oh my god, that's craaazy."

"But of course we all know better these days. Anyway, I just thought I'd let y'all know, cuz a lot of my clients moving in from the West Coast want to know more about the political climate."

"To be honest, my only concern was with Matheus."

"Why? What's wrong with him?"

"He's gay."

"Oh wow! I had no idea!"

I grimace. "Thanks."

"Well rest assured, that won't be a problem at all here. In fact, my friend Darlene has a *pansexual* around your age, if you want me to reach out and connect you two..."

"Actually Matheus is seeing a boy in San Marcos right now. A musician."

"Oh well there you go! Y'all are fitting right in!"

November 2019

San Marcos, Texas

Kai's Apartment

I look over at the throbbing bulge in his shorts as we watch Ru Paul's Drag Race.

"Hey, so, your penis..."

"No I know."

"It's like, very prominent."

"I'm sorry, I'm like constantly hard when I'm around you."

"I feel bad."

"Don't feel bad! I'm totally fine just chilling and watching TV."

"I think you should jerk off or something."

He laughs. "Like, right here in front of you?"

"Yeah, why not? I wanna see what kind of porn you watch."

"Oh god, okay." He grabs his phone. "This is so embarrassing to admit, but I have a subscription to a porn site."

"No!"

"Yeah, I'm one of those people."

"What a chump!"

"Do you want me to show you or not?"

"Yes, oh my god, I'm like bursting with curiosity."

"Okay so first I need to explain what it is, cuz it's kinda weird. Basically every video follows the same narrative. First we're introduced to this macho straight guy, and he's doing this little interview about how macho and straight he is."

"Right. As straight men do."

"And he thinks he's waiting for a girl to show up to shoot this sex scene with, but then this super twinky gay guy shows up instead."

"Plot twist!"

"Yeah. And then the camera guy's like, **welp, if we double your pay, will you fuck him instead?** And the straight guy resists at first, but then they eventually coerce him into it."

"And then they fuck?"

"Yeah, they always end up fucking."

"That's cool."

"No, it's not. I hate it. It's like, weird and homophobic."

"I don't think it's healthy to look at it that way. I mean, literally everyone on the planet has internalized homophobia. I think it's totally natural that it's colored your sexuality to some extent."

"I guess. What about you? Are you into straight guys?"

"Girl, I'm like, exclusively into straight guys."

"Oh, word."

"Okay, I'm ready for this. Show me your favorite video."

"Alright, lemme just pause Drag Race."

"Yeah, what a mood killer."

December 2019

"Matheus! Come here!

I open the back door and stick my head inside. "What is it?"

"Come inside for a second." My mom struggles to pack a blunt over the coffee table.

"I'm smoking a cigarette, what do you want?"

"Goddamnit." She throws the blunt wrap down and wipes the weed crumbs off her lap. "We're running out of weed. It's time for another trip to San Marcos."

"Oh yeah, I forgot to tell you, I'm planning on breaking up with Kai."

"What?"

"Yeah, I just decided I'd rather go without weed for a while than be touched by that man ever again."

"That's really stupid, Matheus."

I snort. "Okay."

"Will you put out your fucking cigarette and come talk to me about this? All the smoke's getting inside."

"No, you come out here. Hoe."

"Jesus Christ." She storms outside and slams the back

door behind her. "So what the fuck is this about breaking up with Kai?"

"Which part did you not understand?"

"I'm just confused, because I thought this little arrangement was working beautifully for everyone. Was it not working beautifully?"

"Mom—"

"You said you liked him, what happened to that?"

"It was kinda fun, and now I'm over it, and that's the end of the conversation."

"Okay so what am I supposed to do now, then? Am I supposed to ask fucking Trixie Pope if she knows any dealers in the area?"

"Yeah, well, maybe you should've thought of that before coming to Texas."

"That's exactly what this is—you're punishing me for wanting to move here."

"I mean, yeah! Maybe I am, bitch! Like, look around you, this isn't working!"

She shakes her head furiously. "This isn't a conversation, Matheus. You're a grown adult, your opinion on where I live has zero weight. Zero. You shouldn't even *be* here right now."

I force a laugh. ***"Shouldn't even be here!*** Wow. So which one is it? Do you need me for weed, or am I a worthless sack of shit to you? It can't be both."

"Right now, you're a worthless sack of shit to me."

"Cool, then that's where we stand."

"So that's your final decision?"

"That's my final decision."

"And you've thought about this long and hard?"

"I have."

"Fine. Then you've lost all your smoking privileges, and the rest of that weed is mine."

"Fine."

December 2019

"Oh my goodness, look at you!" I straighten out his tie. "You look like a beardy little penguin man getting ready for your big orchestra."

"Ew, what the fuck?"

"No, it's cute. You look adorbs, I promise."

He checks his phone. "Fuck, I gotta go."

"Go!"

"You should head out in like 30 minutes cuz there's probably gonna be some traffic around the school. Oh and the admission fee is ten dollars, you remembered that, right?"

"Yeah, I got it. Get outta here."

"Okay. I'll come find you after the show." He kisses me on the cheek.

"Good luck! Don't get a boner on stage!"

"Fuck you, slut!"

—

I slip on one of Kai's hoodies and check myself out in his closet mirror. And then I pull out my phone and block his number.

I kneel in front of a little blue suitcase in his closet and start stuffing handfuls of weed into my hoodie pocket. Slowly at first, and then frantically.

Shit.

I pause, throw a couple of nugs back in, and shut the suitcase.

On my way out of his apartment, I pull a note out of my back pocket and I set it down on the kitchen counter.

Kai,

First of all, I just want to say sorry for not showing up to your orchestra. You probably got really worried when you couldn't find me, and that actually fucking breaks my heart.

I'm breaking up with you, and in the most cowardly way possible. There really isn't a satisfying explanation I could give you. I'm just a terrible person who exploits nice men and then implodes under the weight of my own bullshit and then disappears forever. It's probably a personality disorder. Also I don't have a prefrontal cortex.

I want you to know that everything I said was real. Everything that happened between us was real. You couldn't have been more kind and funny and sexy and interesting. I promise. It's genuinely not worth ruminating on. And tbh it's better this happened sooner rather than later.

Matheus

July 20, 2020

I grab a notecard out of the distortion box.

> *I have a blood clot in my left thigh and it's almost ready to dislodge. It's exactly like that one bitch who died of a heart attack on a flight because she didn't stand up to stretch her legs.*

I hold up the notecard and read it over a few times as a smile creeps across my face, and then I tape it up to my bedroom wall.

I grab another notecard out of the box.

> *The air pressure in my lungs is way too high cuz they're full of particles and that's why I was the only one who felt like my breath was being sucked out when we hit that herb vaporizer bag last summer.*

I tape it up to the wall and grab another notecard.

> *It's not tonsil cancer, it's an infection in my adenoids, and the infected mucus has been dripping down my windpipe and pooling in my lungs for the past two years and one day I suddenly won't be*

able to breathe.
And then they'll have to cut off my foot
Which explains why that cut took three
months to heal
And it was actually just the COPD this
entire time
Cuz the tumor has a tentacle that runs
down my esophagus
And they won't be able to operate because
they'd risk cutting it open
My spit keeps snagging in this one spe-
cific spot
It's hard but it's bendy like this little
cartilaginous beak
Growing directly out of the base of my
tongue
Full of little bloody balls of congealed
pus
And under the flap, there was this row
of blistering nodules
It's exactly like that one bitch
Like something the doctors have never
seen before

I take a step back and admire my collage all at once. I like how it looks in my handwriting. I like seeing them all together, arranged like a web, like how I would actually experience the thought. I think it's the closest thing I've ever made to a self-portrait. And it's so uncanny I can't look away.

July 21, 2020

I sit by the window with my shorts around my ankles and I masturbate furiously to the pool guy.

It's not that I find anything about him particularly attractive. I can't even see his face under his mask and sunglasses and wide-brimmed hat. I guess it's just exciting to think that he could see me. I'm not exactly trying to be discreet about it.

He keeps his head down and drags his net through the water.

July 22, 2020

"And can I get two packs of..."

"Yeah yeah, I know."

"Wait! I'm changing it up today."

"Okay girl, I'm with you."

"What do you recommend? Do you smoke?"

"Um...if you usually go for Lights and you're looking for a little spice, I'd go with 27's. Also cuz they're cheaper."

"Okay, cool. I'll do two packs of 27's."

"Awesome." He grabs the cigarettes and rings them up. "So what is this? What's going on?"

"What do you mean?"

"I've just never seen you so chipper."

"I don't know. Life is good. Lots to be excited about."

"Yeah, like what?"

"Like...I'm writing a book, and I think it's almost done."

"Shut up! That's so cool."

"Thanks." I chuckle. "Yeah it's all kind of coming together now, so."

"What is it about?"

"It's kind of about nothing. Just life happening during a pandemic. Random conversations stitched together."

"Oh."

"Yeah. You're actually in it a couple times. You're probably in it right now."

"What?!" He runs his fingers through his hair. "That's fucking crazy. I suddenly have no idea what to say."

"You can say anything, there's literally no plot. Is there anything you want the world to know?"

"Can I say *fuck?"*

"You can say fuck."

"Um..." He shuts his eyes tight and taps his fingers on the counter. "I don't—I can't think of anything, honestly. Is that okay? You can just delete all this."

"No." I chuckle. "That was perfect."

July 23, 2020

"So how did the exercise go? With the notecards?"

"Oh my god, **loved** it."

"Oh good!"

"It was honestly one of the most life-affirming things I've ever done. Which is funny because all my notecards were about death."

"What was so life-affirming about it?"

"I don't know. Seeing my negative thoughts written out like that—I mean it was just ridiculous. It made me laugh at myself, but in a good way. Like I was funny and interesting and my life was funny and interesting."

Dr. Chinn raises a brow.

"I actually taped them up to my wall. I stare at it all the time."

"Oh wow."

"It's like this deranged stream of consciousness thing, and I'm genuinely into it. Like it excites me on an artistic level. And I know this sounds crazy, but I'm almost **proud** of it."

"Proud of what?"

"Like, proud to have concocted something so absolutely batshit psycho. Is that bad?"

"Um..." Dr. Chinn flips the page on her notepad. "It's not

bad. It's pretty common for people to develop a preciousness for their mental illnesses, but it isn't necessarily problematic in itself as long as you aren't hurting yourself or anyone else. And it doesn't sound like you are."

"Yeah, *preciousness* is definitely the right word for it. And I think I've always had that with my anxiety, but I was too embarrassed to admit it to myself even."

"Right."

"Cuz I'm like, wait, have I been faking my anxiety for the past 22 years? Am I just a fucking attention whore? Has all of this just been an elaborate ploy to look more smart and interesting than I really am? It's wild."

"It's interesting—I don't think there's such a thing as an attention whore. I think when people act a certain way for attention, it means there's an area of their lives that genuinely does need more attention. Does that make sense?"

"Yeah. Damn. Mind blown."

"I think you're on the right track, with everything, with the notecards, with the self-reflection. Don't get so caught up in those feelings of like, *am I doing this wrong?* Because it's an exploration, and that's exactly what you're doing, and there isn't a right or wrong way to go about it."

October 2019

Icy rain blows sideways in our faces as we step out of the bar.

I stick my hands in my pockets and look around. "Do you remember where we parked?"

"This way, I think."

"Wait, hold on." I pull out my pack of cigarettes.

"No, Matheus! I'm fucking freezing!"

"Stop, I'm drunk!"

She crosses her arms and continues down the sidewalk. I stuff my cigarettes back in my pocket and follow.

"Why are you—" *burp*. "Why are you in such an atrocious mood with me today?"

"I'm cold and I just wanna get back to the Airbnb."

"No, you've been pissy with me all day and I demand to know why!"

"Jesus Christ."

"You're so impatient with me. I feel like I can't talk to you about anything anymore."

"We talk all day! That's the fucking problem! And I can't even take a break from you for one second without you getting offended! Like seriously Matheus, fuck off."

"Okay, then maybe I should just *kill myself.*"

She lets out a sharp cackle. "You're a child, I'm so embarrassed for you."

"No!" I pull on her arm.

"Don't fucking grab me like that."

"You can't talk to me like that! I'm not gonna let you get away with it!"

"Lower your voice! People are staring."

I let go of her arm. "I don't give a fuck."

"Let's just go, okay? I'm tired."

"Don't talk to me."

"Mhmm."

—

"Mom, stop the car!"

She pounds on the breaks halfway up the driveway. "Shit, Matheus. What is it?"

"Look!" I point at Kita and Lily sitting out on the porch steps in the rain, the front door swung wide open behind them.

"What the—?"

We get out of the car and the dogs come running down the driveway to greet us with wagging tails.

"Holy shit." I pick up Kita and she licks my face frantically. "I can't believe they didn't run away! I'm fucking shook."

"Matheus, get back in the car."

"Why?"

"There might be someone inside. I'm dead serious."

"You think so? I think the dogs would be freaking the fuck out. It was probably just Kita jumping up on the doorknob like she always does."

"No, I have a weird feeling about this. We need to get back in the car and wait for the police."

"Nah, I'm good actually. I'm gonna go inside check it out with Kita."

"Matheus, stop!"

"It's fine! I'm the perfect amount of drunk for this."

I set Kita down in the foyer and turn on the lights. "Hello?"
No response.

I look around as I head down the hall. "Hello, home invader? You can come out now! I'm unarmed and I want to die!"

Nothing.

I swing into my room and peek behind the door. "I'm right here you cowardly piece of shit!"

"Matheus? Where are you?"

"I'm in my room! It's fine, this home invader's a fucking pussy!" I kick open my bathroom door. "Come on, bitch, it's a free homicide!"

"What in the fuck is going on, Matheus? You're scaring me."

I rip back my shower curtain. "Look, Mom. It's nothing. There's no one here."

She stares back at me wide-eyed.

"Did you hear me? I said there's no one fucking here!"

"I heard you! Jesus! What's wrong with you?"

"Fuck." I grab my stomach and crawl into the bathtub.

"You overdid it."

"Shut up, please, shut the fuck up."

"Okay. Do you need anything?"

"Just go away, please. And turn off the lights."

September 2019

"Moules marinières?"

I raise my hand. "Ici."

"And for you, mademoiselle, moules à l'ardennaise."

"Thank you so much."

"Et voilà." He lifts the lids off our cast-iron pots, revealing a steaming bed of mussels in broth. "Bon appétit."

We gawk at our food and chuckle a little.

"Wow."

"No, Mom, like you don't even understand. I'm so in my element right now."

She raises her glass. "Cheers."

"Cheers, bitch. To Palm Springs living." *Clink*

—

The waiter takes our bowl of discarded shells. "Can I twist anyone's arm for a look at the dessert menu?"

"Yes, two dessert menus please! No arm twisting required."

"Of course, mademoiselle."

"Mm." I set down my wine glass. "When we get out of here, I'm aboutta have the best cigarette of my life."

"I bet."

"Mom. Look at me, Mom. ***This could be our lives!*** This restaurant could be our ***spot!*** Can you imagine?"

"No." She waves her hand dismissingly. "I told you not to get too excited, Matheus. I have no intention of moving to Palm Springs."

"Well why the fuck not?"

"It just doesn't make sense. It's too expensive, it's in the middle of the desert—can you imagine ***utility bills*** in the fucking desert? No, of course you can't."

"That's bullshit. Tell me you're not happy right now."

"Well of course I'm happy, this place is paradise. But it's a resort town, I can't afford to spend the rest of my life here with you on some permanent vacation. I'm sorry, that's not how the world works."

"What about your stocks?"

"What stocks?"

"The ***stocks?*** And the bonds?"

She laughs.

"I'm not even kidding, I refuse to live anywhere else. Do you know how many times I've had to check my faggotry in the last three days? Zero. Zero times. Look: I can do whatever I want with my wrists and nobody's even gonna look twice. How incredible is that?"

"You're ridiculous."

July 28, 2020

My mom climbs into the car and scowls. "It smells like cigarettes in here."

"Nice to see you, too. How was your flight?"

"I have a headache."

"Alrighty." I put the car in drive and peel away from the curb. "Do you want something to drink? I think there's a Vitamin Water in the back seat..."

"I'm fine, I just need to get home and take a shower. Have you seriously been smoking in my car?"

"No, that's just me. That's just what I smell like."

"Mm." She rolls down her window.

—

"Home sweet home!" I lug her suitcase inside as the dogs jump up on our shins. "I spent all day cleaning, I think you'll be pleasantly surprised—"

"What the fuck is all this, Matheus?" She rips a notecard off the wall. *"Pulmonary embolism?"*

"Oh, it's an exercise I've been doing for Dr. Chinn! It's like, every conceivable way I could die. Or just random things that get stuck in my brain."

"Blistering little tumors on my adenoids blocking the

airflow...what the fuck?"

I cackle. "Isn't it hilarious? That's the whole point—when I see it written out like this, it just sounds so ridiculous!"

"No, Matheus. You're taking this down."

"No I know. I just wanted you to see it before I took it down, cuz I think it's kinda cool."

"Is this on every wall in the house?"

"No, just my room and the hallway. And my bathroom. And some of the kitchen cabinets."

"I just—I can't. I'm gonna go take a shower and lay down. This needs to go tonight."

July 29, 2020

"Tell me a story about Tennessee. You haven't told me any stories yet."

My mom clicks her lighter furiously. "Shit, Matheus, where did all my lighters go? I swear I had like four good lighters out here!"

"They're around here somewhere. Maybe in random pockets? Look, it works though."

"Yeah, but it's shit. I don't have the patience for shitty lighters."

"Mm." I sit back and watch her cautiously. "Is everything okay? Like, did something happen in Tennessee?"

"No, Tennessee was great. Really really great, actually. Exactly what I needed."

"Okay, I just—I thought I'd ask because you've been in a terrifying mood since coming back, so."

"Okay, fine. You wanna know why I've been in a bad mood?"

"Um, yeah."

"It's not about Tennessee. It's because there's something I need to tell you, and I know you're gonna have a big reaction, so I'm just preemptively pissed off at you for making my life so difficult."

"Just tell me. I promise I'm not gonna flip out."

"Didier's coming back on the 1st."

I smirk. "No."

"Yes."

"You're fucking with me."

"Why would I be fucking with you?"

"But this doesn't make any sense. It's like something that would happen in a dream."

"You knew he was coming back eventually."

"I mean yeah, **eventually**, but I assumed something would have to change first. Right? Or else it's gonna be just like before, and then why did we even go through the trouble?"

"I don't know what you were expecting to happen."

"Yeah, me neither. Damn."

"So, okay, it's done. And you promised me you wouldn't have a big reaction."

"I won't. It's done."

—

"So...about Didier coming back."

"Yeah?"

"I'm sorry, I know you don't wanna talk about it, but I think we should have a conversation about how this is gonna work."

"What do you mean?"

"Like, what is your role gonna be in all this?"

"My role? I don't have a role."

"It's just—I've been doing really well lately. Like, really uncharacteristically well. And I wanna keep that going for as long as possible."

"Great, then do that."

"Yeah but like, my well-being around Didier is gonna require you to...step up."

She laughs.

"It's not funny though. Like you sprung this news on me, and I think I should have a say in how this is gonna go down."

"But that's the thing, Matheus, you don't get a say. It's my house, I can do whatever the fuck I want."

I wince. "Oh wow. Was that as nauseating to say as it was to hear?"

"I think we're done now."

"Okay. Lovely chatting with you as always."

July 30, 2020

"I brought something for you." My mom unzips her suitcase. "I was gonna give this to you yesterday, but you were in one of your tense moods."

"Ah."

She pulls out a Ziploc bag full of little rose-colored crystals. "Aren't they pretty? I thought you'd appreciate them."

"Holy shit, where did you find this?" I take the bag and massage it in my hands.

"They were all over the ranch. Like, right on the surface."

"This is really cool, thank you."

"You're welcome."

"Did you bring anything for Didier?"

She ignores me and goes back to unpacking her suitcase.

"Huh? Anything for Didier?"

"No, Matheus, I didn't bring anything for Didier."

"That's a shame."

—

"Matheus come here!"

"What!"

"Come here! I need to show you something in your bathroom!"

"What is it?"

"Tell me the truth, was Leggy here while I was gone?"

"No! What the fuck?"

"Well this sink's been used."

"So what? Sometimes I use that sink."

"Mm." She steps into my shower and holds up a Pantene hair mask. "And I'm supposed to believe that this is yours?"

"No, it's Leggy's, but it's from that last time she was here."

"She was here over a month ago, Matheus. I've cleaned this shower since then and I know for a fact that this wasn't in here."

"No no NO!" I slap the bathroom counter. "You're not LISTENING!"

"Calm down. What are you doing?"

"No, what are YOU doing? Why are you looking for bullshit reasons to get mad at me?"

"Matheus, I know you're back on Vyvanse. I noticed it the second I got back."

"OH MY GOD NO I'M NOT! I SWEAR TO GOD, FUCKING DRUG TEST ME!"

"It's okay. Look, I'm not mad. I'm just worried, because it's starting to look a lot like last time—"

"YOU'RE FUCKING RETARDED IF YOU THINK I'M TWEAKING!"

She puts her hands up in surrender and walks away. I follow her out of the bathroom.

"Stop!" I grab her arm. "You can't just accuse me of that and then walk away!"

"Don't restrain me."

"I'm not restraining you, I just need you to listen!" My voice cracks and I let out a sharp sob. *"Just fucking listen!"*

"Jesus Christ, look at you. You're **sick,** Matheus."

I double over and grab my stomach and scream all the air out of me.

"Stop it! Oh my god, *stop!"*

I grab a glass on the counter and hurl it at the wall with all my strength. And when it shatters, something else in the room also shatters, and suddenly I feel uncomfortably sober, and stupid, and embarrassed.

My mom covers her mouth in shock as she tip-toes around the broken glass and crouches down to survey the damage to the wall.

"I can't have this, Matheus."

"I know."

"I need you out of the house before Didier gets back."

I nod.

"I'm sorry, but I don't trust you not to start shit."

Tears well in my eyes as I continue nodding. "Yeah."

"Go get the broom, please, before the dogs step in this."

November 2017

"You might've noticed a new face in our circle this morning. This is Annette, everyone say hi."

"Hi Annette."

"Today is actually her 19th birthday, so, happy birthday Annette. Welcome."

"Thank you. Thrilled to be here."

"So let me just explain how this is gonna work. This is our status meeting, it's how we start every morning. Everyone fills out this little mental health survey and then we go around the circle reporting our answers. You'll notice at the bottom we have a gratitude section where you can list a couple things you're grateful for or just something you're looking forward to. Make sure you do that."

"Okay."

"But since you're new, we're gonna start by letting you introduce yourself and tell us a little more about what brings you here."

"Right now?"

"Yeah, if you're comfortable with that."

"Sure." Annette clears her throat. "Ok so, hi, I'm Annette. Scorpio babies represent. Um...I know I'm younger than a lot of you, but this is actually my third time being institutionalized, so, watch out."

I snort.

"No, but seriously...I'm here for anxiety. Mostly health anxiety. It started when I was in 4th grade and I thought I had Lyme disease or heavy metal poisoning or something cuz I was tired all the time and everything felt like a simulation. So my parents took me to like every endocrinologist in Seattle, and it turns out I'm actually just crazy. But I've never really accepted that hypothesis, and I keep finding more and more shit wrong with me, and...I don't know. It's kinda hard to find the motivation to do anything when you're convinced that you're dying. So. Here I am. And my survey answers are...4, 7, 2, 4, and I'm grateful for my dog Marshmallow. Is that enough?"

—

"Hi, Annette, can I sit with you?"

"Sure!"

I sit down next to her on the courtyard bench and unwrap my sandwich. "What'd you get? Hummus plate?"

"Yeah. It was a lot better on paper."

"Yeah, that's a classic mistake. The sandwiches are where it's at."

"Which one did you get?"

"Chicken salad. But they're all good, I've tried all of them."

"Good to know. What was your name again?"

"Matheus."

"I don't think I heard you share today."

"No yeah I'm kind of over it at this point. Tomorrow's my last day."

"Oh nice."

"I just wanted to say, like, you're my favorite person here and I'm sad that we're not gonna get to be rehab sisters."

"Oh no! Were you my rehab sister?"

"Like, you have no idea. These suicidal-depressive bitches cannot keep up."

She laughs.

"I also have pretty bad health anxiety, by the way. It's not really why I'm here, but, it was really refreshing to hear your share."

"Oh nice! What's like, your main health thing?"

"For me it's mostly cardiovascular stuff and mouth stuff. But I'm a smoker, so, fuck me."

"Dude yeah, I can totally relate to that. Like, manifesting the illness."

"Right because who the fuck else is gonna manifest it? Not those bitch-ass doctors, that's for sure."

She laughs.

"Dude it's actually so nice to talk to someone who understands this particular brand of insanity, in the flesh. I've never had that before."

"Yeah, me neither. I mean I've been on forums and stuff, but..."

"Yeah, same. But I think this is what it's all about. Like, being able to joke about it."

"Totally."

"Actually, can I?—Can I get your number? Would that

be weird?"

"No, not at all!"

"Okay, cool." I hand her my phone. "I'm gay, by the way, so this isn't me trying to come on to you or anything."

"No yeah, I'm very aware. The whole **rehab sister** thing definitely sealed the deal."

"Right." I chuckle. "Do you smoke weed?"

"God no, that shit wrecks me."

"Ugh, I feel you. I hate being high, I don't know why I keep insisting on it."

She hands me back my phone. "Here you go."

"Okay, perfect. I'll text you my name cuz I'm sure you've already forgotten it. But yeah. Feel free to hit me up whenever you're spiraling or whatever, and we can talk about normal things. Lighten the mood. I have an endless supply of patience for this shit."

"Oh my god, I'd love that!" She smiles down at her phone. "And same goes for you, by the way."

"Okay, cool. It's a deal."

July 31, 2020

"Good morning!"

"Hi, Dr. Chinn."

"Where are you? Are you in your car?"

"Yeah." I hold up my phone and pan it around. "I'm at a Denny's parking lot in Riverside right now. Can you hear me over the AC?"

"Yeah, I can hear you. Why are you at a Denny's parking lot in Riverside?"

"Well...funny story. My mom kind of temporarily kicked me out, so, I'm heading to Orange County to stay with a friend for a few days."

"Oh my god, what happened?"

"I don't even know. She's convinced that I'm back on Vyvanse for some reason? And then she dropped the bomb that Didier's coming back literally tomorrow, and we like couldn't even have a proper conversation about it, and I ended up getting so frustrated that I threw a glass at the wall. So yeah. She told me she doesn't trust me around Didier, she thinks I'm gonna snap at him or something. Isn't that funny? The thought of me just snapping at someone unprovoked?"

She shakes her head. "I'm so sorry."

"It's okay, the derealization hit me **hard** last night, so now I'm just like on autopilot and it's fine. And it'll be this way for a while, and that's fine too. I'm kind of over this fucking book anyway."

She blinks back at me.

"Actually—can I light a cigarette? Would that be weird?"

"Go for it."

"Cool, thanks." I roll down my window and light a cigarette. "Oh my god, this is instantly so much better. Smoking in therapy, what a concept."

"So why does your mom think you're back on Vyvanse?"

"Um, I don't know, cuz she's a dumb whore?" I take a furious drag of my cigarette. "I'm always a little manic coming off a depressive episode, this is nothing new. I think it's just easier for her to call me a drug addict and push me away than actually have to deal with this Didier mess."

"Right."

"I'll be honest with you, Dr. Chinn, I'm not really looking to get therapized today."

"Oh, okay."

"Yeah, I'm really sorry. This was more of a courtesy call to let you know that I'm gonna be mentally checked out for a while. I just didn't want to straight-up ghost you."

"I understand."

"Fuck." I wipe at my forehead. "I'm such an asshole."

"Listen, you have nothing to apologize for. If your battery's at zero, then your battery's at zero, and I would never advise you to push past that."

"Yeah. I just feel bad, because you've been so great, and

I'm not even pretending to try anymore. I'm such a lazy piece of shit."

She furrows her brows.

"We could sit here and come up with a million excuses for why I'm so tired, but I'm starting to think maybe I'm just **weak.** Spoiled, arrogant, lazy, and weak. Maybe it's just that simple."

"Well—"

"I don't think I have the right to be exhausted like this. I literally just sit at home all day watching TV and waiting to die. I actually forget that we're in a pandemic all the time, cuz this is pretty much what my life was like before. How pathetic is that?"

"What do you want?"

"I want to wake the fuck up. I want to move out of my mom's house."

"Mhmm."

"I blame her for a lot this, for me not being able to handle the most basic things."

"Right."

"I mean, the first time we got fucked up together, I was 14. It was actually right after my 8th grade graduation, we got home and she made me a celebratory caipirinha because I was officially a high schooler." I chuckle. "God, what a dumb bitch. She didn't care what it was doing to me, what it was doing to my future, she just wanted a drinking buddy, you know? A live-in drinking buddy."

"Why do you think she made you her drinking buddy?"

"Because...I was there. I was the **only** one there. She lost everyone after she divorced my dad, all her married friends. You think I'm exaggerating, but I'm not. Cuz people only saw this hysterical woman ripping her perfect little family apart, but they didn't see all the things my dad was doing to push her to that point behind closed doors. But *I* knew. I believed her, cuz I was there. And my dad—he was just starting to realize that I was gay, and he was doing everything in his passive-aggressive power to prevent that from happening. I needed to get the fuck out of that house too, you know? So that was like, a really intense trauma bond. Us against the world. Fuck everyone else, fuck men, fuck the patriarchy. The drinking and drugging just kind of fit like a glove on top of all that."

"You were just trying to be there for your mom."

"Yeah. And I think that's where the resentment comes in, because I feel like I did so much for her during those years. We moved out together, bought a house together, figured it all out together. I mean, she got married when she was 22 and my dad never let her handle any money, she had no idea what the fuck she was doing. And I was there, you know? I would drop everything when she was upset, sit with her for hours while she cried, just feeling her pain so deeply like it was my own pain. And I was fucking 12, so that was like way above and beyond. And now it's like, well where's the same effort for me when it's *my* life blowing up? Where's the same patience and understanding? It's not there. I'm still just the drinking buddy."

Dr. Chinn sits back and sighs.

"But it's crazy to think that was ten years ago. Ten years we've been living like this, just giving the middle finger to the world. I'm over it, it's time to move on, it's time to level up. I don't need her like that anymore, you know?"

"Right. And I'm pretty sure she doesn't need you to keep

protecting her, either."

"Yeah. Goddamnit, Dr. Chinn, you just therapized me."

She laughs. "Hey, you did all the talking!"

"I did, didn't I? Fuck." I toss my cigarette out the window and light another. "How about this, I'll stay for one more cigarette and then I'll go."

"Whatever you need."

"Okay, cool. Let's talk about something fun now, like death. I've been itching to talk about death all week."

"Death it is, then."

"So I have this new cancer symptom I'd like to dump on you, but I don't want you to make any facial expressions no matter how shocked and appalled you are."

She clicks her pen.

"So yeah, anyway, it all started a few nights ago when I felt a pop in my ribs."